DORSET IN THE FIRST WORLD WAR

DORSET
IN THE
FIRST WORLD WAR

Rodney Legg

DORSET BOOKS

First published in Great Britain in 2012

British Library Cataloguing-in-Publication Data
A CIP record for this title is available from the British Library

ISBN 978 1 871164 91 6

DORSET BOOKS
Dorset Books is a Partnership Between
Dorset County Council & Halsgrove

Halsgrove House,
Ryelands Business Park,
Bagley Road, Wellington, Somerset TA21 9PZ
Tel: 01823 653777   Fax: 01823 216796
email: sales@halsgrove.com

Part of the Halsgrove group of companies
Information on all Halsgrove titles is available at: www.halsgrove.com

Printed and bound in the UK by TJ International Ltd

Contents

Foreword

HAVING GROWN UP among memories of the Second World War, and documented them in a series of books culminating in *Dorset at War*, I used to regard the Great War – as my uncles called it – as an unfathomable anachronism. For decades it had been denied its place in the national psyche if only through embarrassment at the futile carnage that had solved nothing.

The cause of European political implosion defies rational explanation. It became an inevitability once the Triple Entente aligned France, Russia and Britain against Imperial Germany. The catalyst was the assassination by an anarchist of Archduke Franz Ferdinand in Sarajevo on 28 June 1914, though few realised the significance at the time. Management of the resultant conflict was tawdry until Lloyd George gave direction where Asquith had faltered. Likewise the rise of Haig after the death of Kitchener. The Second World War, for all its inherent brutality, had the saving graces of excitement, mobility and Winston Churchill (who learnt lessons from round one). It also passed the morality test, as set by St Thomas Aquinas, for 'a just war'.

To my lasting disappointment, I missed the opportunities for interviewing local uncle Frank Watts from Bournemouth – who was gassed at Ypres and gave me his souvenirs from the trenches – and Kent uncle Bill Bennett who lovingly stripped down the 1915-made Lee-Enfield I gave him one Christmas. He declared it the 'best rifle ever made' and fixed the bayonet to demonstrate how it use it. That was by turning the blade sideways against my tummy – to break the victim's ribs – and facilitate quick extraction. To Aunt Effie, in Moordown, and Aunt Iris, at Rochester, the words of the song applied... 'they'll never tell you'. That suited both women. For childhood me, however, there was a spate of stories, with bathos and blood and guts punctuating endless wallowing and waiting in filth for something to happen.

Many of their experiences are here, through carbon-copy memories of others, and similarly those of Canford School's teacher in a flying-machine. I chatted to Lieutenant Yvone Kirkpatrick of the Royal Flying Corps in his seaside villa looking out across Ringstead Bay, but at least Michael Moynihan proceeded to scoop up his story in *A Place Called Armageddon*. This 'Intrepid Birdman' appears in my pages by proxy, through the similar amazing story of Louis Arbon Strange, who had the contemporary Dorset connections. Like Kirkpatrick, it was only after the war that Lawrence of Arabia adopted Dorset, so he too has to be excluded.

The catalyst for this book was a cherished late-life memory of meeting Harry Patch, from Fonthill in Wiltshire, who was the sole survivor of the millions who had fought in the trenches on the Western Front. His biography had been ghost-written by Richard van Emden as *The Last Fighting Tommy*. My contribution, after Harry's passing, was a memorial paragraph in *The Times*. From that I realised I now had to tell what I knew, or had found out and filed from primary and secondary sources over several decades, whilst there was still time. It coincided with my personal pilgrimage to the battlefields from Mons to the Somme.

The bonus is that much of what happened in Dorset during the First World War turns out to have been either directly or indirectly due to the ideas and enthusiasms of Winston Churchill.

one

Mobilisation of the Fleet

THE ROYAL NAVY'S First Fleet – about to be designated the Grand Fleet – had been sailing and training in the English Channel since gathering for a review at Spithead by King George V on 17 July 1914. They moved northward, for what became the Great War, from Portland Harbour on Wednesday 29 July. Lines of battleships secretly slipped from their moorings that evening on the orders of Winston Churchill, the First Lord of the Admiralty. At speed, without lights and maintaining radio silence, they were to steam for the safety of Scapa Flow in the Orkney Islands.

Churchill feared that Portland was vulnerable to a surprise attack by motor-torpedo boats. Operational ships were to be at their war stations, before a declaration of war, 'therefore if possible before we had decided ourselves'. Those were Churchill's own words. He later described the unfolding events in Dorset which he successfully concealed both from the German High Command in Berlin and the British Cabinet in Whitehall:

King George V (left) on HMS Orion in a pre-war Fleet review at Portland.

The Fleet at anchor off Weymouth.

Clockwise (l to r): Peacetime sailors from Portland heading on leave to Weymouth Station.

Last picnic on Chesil Beach, between Wyke Regis and Portland, in July 1914.

Ratings relax as a boat circles the 5th Battle Squadron in Portland Harbour.

Clearing personal trunks from HMS Agamemnon *as she was put on a war footing in Portland Harbour, July 1914.*

'We may now picture this great fleet with its flotillas of cruisers steaming slowly out of Portland Harbour, squadron by squadron, scores of gigantic castles of steel wending their way across the misty, shining sea, like giants bowed in anxious thought. We may picture them again as darkness fell, 18 miles of warships running at high speed and in absolute darkness, through the narrow Straits, bearing with them into the North Sea the safeguard of considerable affairs. The strategic concentration of the fleet had been achieved with its transfer to Scottish waters.'

The Navy's Second Fleet had already dispersed from Portland, at noon on Monday 27 July, mainly to training establishments around the country, though the Dreadnought *Bellerophon* was en route to a dry-dock in Gibraltar. During the previous week, personal effects were removed and put into store at the dockyard, though much would

Taking off personal trunks from the battleship HMS Agamemnon into a gear-boat at Portland, July 1914.

Below: '1A' labels on barrels of cordite, the propellant charge for naval shells, being loaded on to HMS Agamemnon *at Portland in July 1914.*

Inspection of midshipmen on HMS Agamemnon, in the process of loading cordite in Portland Harbour, in July 1914.

*'Completing' with projectiles -
13.5-inch shells being prepared
for action on HMS
Agamemnon, July 1914.*

Left: *Shells in the foreground
and barrels of cordite behind
during the arming of the guns
on HMS* Agamemnon.

Right: *Continuing 'completing'
by taking on board a torpedo in
the arming of HMS* Agamemnon.

never be needed again. Red flags flew as ammunition was taken on board, including Dorset-made projectiles from Whitehead Torpedo Company at Wyke Regis. Frenetic activity succeeded in readying the warships in a matter of days.

The old battleship HMS *Prince of Wales* was the only capital ship remaining at Portland. She was taking on coal in the harbour when the signal came through from the Admiralty that began the Great War. Everyone cheered, ratings recalled, before they resumed coaling with renewed vigour. Issued at 23.00 hours on Tuesday 4 August 1914, and effective from midnight, the message read:

> *'Commence hostilities against Germany.'*

His Majesty's Ships Russell,
Exmouth, Cornwallis *and*
Duncan *leaving Portland for
Scapa Flow.*

The first loss of the war was due to that old enemy – the weather – rather than the Germans. The 6,010-ton ironclad battleship HMS *Invincible*, demoted by the Admiralty and re-named *Fisgard II* upon re-use of her historic name, was under tow from Portsmouth with the tugs *Danube* and *Southampton*, on 17 September 1914. As she took on increasing

The white ensign stiff in the air as the last church service of peacetime is held on the stern of HMS Agamemnon.

quantities of water, the 'scratch crew' carried everything moveable from upper to lower decks, in an attempt to restore stability. It was to no avail. Five miles off Portland Bill, at 17.09 hours, the former warship heeled and lay on her beam-ends. Her four ship's boats and 24 lifeboats were available for an orderly evacuation but things did not go well. Only 43 of the complement survived. The other 21 men drowned.

Fears of German motor-torpedo boat or submarine incursions into Portland Harbour had already led to attempts at sealing the entrances with nets. The first version comprised thousands of small, round glass bulbs in floating cases. These were

Back at Portland for HMS Agamemnon's 'Torture Party' of 'Xmas 1914' sending 'Best wishes for a Happy New Year from us all'.

Loading a 21-inch torpedo into an H-class submarine at Portland.

suspended on piano wire, with the idea that they would 'bob about' if activated by an intruder, but it was soon realised that by that time it would probably be too late to react.

The Victorian battleship HMS Hood selected for scuttling as an anti-submarine obstacle at Portland.

HMS Hood in place to block the South Ship Channel into Portland Harbour.

The next development was torpedo nets, hanging like curtains across the channel, suspended from floats known as 'cats'. Tom Pike, who was at Portland at the time, understood that the arrangement worked well for the north and east entrances but failed at the South Ship Channel when the main tide flowed out from the harbour. There the nets ran sideways 'like drapes in the wind'. Five-ton anchors, called 'clumps', were attached to the bottom of the nets to overcome the problem.

However the experts had reckoned without the immense quantities of rubbish which float away from a fleet base. This jetsam caused havoc, Tom Pike told me:

'The nets were clogged, and at full tide they naturally flattened with the stream and lay useless on the surface, despite their heavy anchors. It used to be said that you could walk on the nets where they filled with gash.'

Cables and the keel of the Hood, *sunk to block Portland's South Ship Channel on 4 November 1914.*

The Admiralty decided there was no time for further experimentation. The southern entrance into Portland Harbour was to be abandoned and blocked. This would be achieved by sinking an obsolete battleship. Selected for scuttling was the redundant iron-clad HMS *Hood*, 14,000 tons, which went down on 4 November 1914.

The intention was that she would be raised after the war, but salvage was never attempted, and the hull and crushed superstructure are still there today. She had 'turned turtle' with her bilge keel showing above the surface at low water. Tom Pike explained that in about 1960 the masts and funnels of the *Hood* were no longer capable of supporting her upside-down weight:

Whitehead Torpedo Works at Wyke Regis, Weymouth.

'They snapped and the big whale-back of her hull sank from sight. She must be lying on her gunwales.'

In January 1915, William S. Edwards of The Gables at West Allington, Bridport, principal owner of the net manufacturers Messrs W. Edwards & Son, was summoned to London for a conference with Winston Churchill, as First Lord of the Admiralty, and Sir John 'Jackie' Fisher, the First Sea Lord. Churchill said that the only thing that could possibly defeat the Royal Navy was the submarine, and with the loss of the Navy there would be the probability of losing the war. He explained that a naval officer had thought of using steel-wire nets for catching submarines, in precisely the same way as nets were used for catching herrings, the only difference being the use of steel-wire cable instead of hemp ropes. A specification was drawn up for an Indicator (Anti-Submarine) Net which was made in Bridport.

Dorset-made Whitehead torpedo.

two

Building a Cordite Factory

THE SECOND ORDER to impact upon Dorset, from Winston Churchill as First Lord of the Admiralty, was the building of a Royal Naval Cordite Factory. Cordite is the propellant for the Navy's guns but its production was in private hands. Churchill was insistent that in order to improve ballistics and ensure an adequate independent supply the process required nationalisation. The distinguished chemical engineer Colonel Sir Frederic Nathan (1861-1933) was seconded from the Nobel Explosives Company's Ardeer factory, to oversee construction of a modern purpose-built works, for the Admiralty.

Where to put such a volatile concern was the next question. Malcolm Bowditch, in his study *Cordite-Poole* (its telegraphic address), shows that the remote location of uninhabited heathland beside a undisturbed backwater of Poole Harbour was key to Holton Heath being chosen from a short-list of contenders. The problem lay in the ingredients rather than the finished product. A dense clear liquid called nitro-glycerine (NG) had to be mixed with a fibrous, solid guncotton. Both are hazardous and explosive. Holton Heath also met requirements in being a split-level but low-lying site, with an adequate water supply (from a riverside pumping station at Corfe Mullen), and an easily dug sandy sub-soil. It was between a main road and the London and South Western Railway. The sea could be reached by a short siding to Rocklea Jetty. The destination was to be Priddy's Hard, Gosport, and Upnor at Rochester, Kent.

The land in Dorset was bought from Sir John Lees of Post Green, Lytchett Minster. Consulting engineers were Sir Douglas Fox and Partners and the construction company Topham, Jones and Railton from London. Mann Egerton Limited and Sturtivant Limited constructed the intricate complex of chemical drains, pipework and troughs. Malcolm Bowditch records labour unrest, culminating in a strike, which was broken by soldiers from Worgret Camp, Wareham, appearing with fixed bayonets.

There were inevitable spy stories linked to the fate of those foreign nationals who were subjected to court martial and taken to the Tower of London to face the firing squad. MI5 records show that a total of 65 German agents were arrested and convicted, mostly being imprisoned, under the Aliens Restriction Act. German sources claim they sent upwards of 120 agents though it was admitted that from many nothing was ever heard. At Holton Heath a 'prohibited zone' was established around the huge construction site as sabotage fears grew, after the German Sektion-P success in blowing up the ammunition dump at Black Tom Pier, New Jersey, on 30 July 1916. The Metropolitan Police manned a monitoring post opposite Heathwood Garage at the Holton Heath cross-roads.

Basic training for the first workers was provided by the Royal Gunpowder Factory at Waltham Abbey, Essex. The acid factory at Holton Heath came into use in 1916. Most of its pressure vessels were of lead which brought its own hazards. From this time the police were also required to give advance warning of thunder storms. Six blasts of the siren, each of four seconds duration, would send men scurrying from the NG and guncotton mixing rooms to the security of 'clean' buildings. Steam-powered saddle-tank engines worked the approaches but the narrow-gauge lines threading the site were the preserve of safer paraffin-fuelled locomotives. Buildings in sensitive areas were initially timber-clad with rubberoid-coated corrugated iron roofs, though concrete and asbestos became the norm.

To minimise the repercussions of any accident, each workplace was separated from the next by berms and bunds of protective landscaping, with the result that the operation spread across several hundred acres, taking up the entire view from Black Hill. All was inside 12-feet high black-painted railings.

three

The Royal Naval Division at Blandford

CHURCHILL'S THIRD DECISION that affected Dorset was to establish a Royal Naval Division, which was formed at Walmer, Kent, in September 1914. This was created as a Marine Brigade, which was in effect a land Army, to deal with the problem of mobilisation having put 25,000 Naval reservists into uniform. Such numbers were far in excess of additional manpower needed for the ships of the Royal Navy. To the horror of many volunteers, though promised a 'mobile' role, they found themselves trained to join 'the poor bloody infantry' rather than going to sea.

Having originally landed in Antwerp, to defend the Channel ports, the German advance saw them hastily withdrawn to England. Their training depot was at the Crystal Palace in London. Temporary accommodation for the men was found at Chatham (Anson Battalion), Portsmouth (Nelson Battalion), Portland (Howe Battalion) and Plymouth (Hood Battalion). For a permanent base, Churchill chose Blandford Racecourse on chalk downland east of the market town, on the foothills of the Dorset Downs. The first arrivals from Portsmouth, to march a mile into a tented city, arrived at Blandford Station on 27 November 1914. Luckier arrivals, from the Marine Brigade, were found lodgings in the town and surrounding villages.

Their General Officer Commanding, Major-General (Sir) Archibald Paris (1861-1937), set up his staff headquarters in the Stud House at Pimperne. The whole of the countryside uphill from the railway, along chalky Black Lane, became a construction site with dozens of steam traction engines and hundreds of horse-drawn carts. Major Alan Harfield, in his book *Blandford and the Military* (1984), describes the evolution of the hutted encampment. Lines of wooden billets were numbered A1 to A4, B1 to B4 and C1 to C4. Each group had its own ablution blocks and mess-rooms. There was also a cluster of communal facilities including a canteen, medical unit, YMCA, and Church of England and Methodist churches.

As the camp expanded, its brigades were reformed, though still named for famous admirals. The 1st Brigade comprised the Benbow, Drake, Hawke and Nelson battalions. The 2nd Brigade, Royal Naval Division, comprised the Anson, Collingwood, Hood and Howe battalions. Training took place across Dorset, such as at Symondsbury, where trenches were dug in January, in an authentic coastal location adjoining Thorncombe Beacon and looking across to Golden Cap. Bridport reporter John Rowson wrote:

> 'There are 1,000 fine, smart young fellows. They are digging elaborate entrenchments on Eype Down, skilfully laid out from five to six feet deep, in zig-zag formation. Whole days are spent in the trenches, exactly as in the fighting line, with cooking done under service conditions, and no man showing himself as snipers represent the enemy. On Sundays the trenches are visited by crowds of town and country people. The men are looking forward to renewing "auld acquaintance" with the town where they spent such pleasant days in their training.'

Postcard from the Young Men's Christian Association.

Departures from Blandford began on 1 February 1915 – for Plymouth and 'a secret destination'. The Nelson Battalion was seen off in the pouring rain, as they filed through Blandford on 17 February, by Winston Churchill. He was back again a week later, this time accompanied by King George V, and the remainder of the men had left by the end of the month. The ghost camp became the divisional depot as its men sailed towards Egypt.

Churchill, as First Lord of the Admiralty, had persuaded the War Council to back his adventure at Gallipoli in the Dardanelles. It had been under consideration since 25 November 1914. The aim was to utilise British seapower to establish a second front in what was naively regarded as 'the soft underbelly of the Mediterranean' and to bring about the fall of Constantinople. The Navy was to secure the waters of the Dardanelles so that land forces could invade the Gallipoli peninsula. Turkey was Germany's ally and its stranglehold of the Black Sea threatened Tsarist Russia. This diversion in the Dardanelles promised a break-through against the Central Powers, in a refreshing attempt to regain the initiative, as the great armies fought themselves to a standstill in the carnage of the Western Front.

Reality was different. The Turkish forts gave stubborn resistance. Trench warfare in Gallipoli became a hot, sandy mirror-image of the military stalemate in the mud of Flanders. It ended in failure with the withdrawal causing resignations of the First Sea Lord, Admiral Sir Jackie Fisher, and his political master, Winston Churchill.

The secret evacuation from the Gallipoli misadventure was masterminded by Old Shirburnian General Sir Charles Munro (who arrived at Sherborne from Australia as an

11-year-old in 1871). He commanded the 2nd Division in 1914 and the 3rd Army in 1915 before:

> '... *being handed the poisoned chalice of Commander-in-Chief, Eastern Mediterranean.*'

His despatch to London sealed the death-knell to Churchill's bold initiative. Even if the forces pinned down in the Dardanelles could secure their positions there was no possibility of an advance to Constantinople. Therefore, as no purpose was served by remaining, it was sensible to leave. The solution he devised for extricating the Allies from landing beaches under the enemy guns was to continue the appearance of normal working for as long as possible, whilst at the same time withdrawing all reserve forces and materials, and then to pull out 'remaining units as speedily as possible'. Having accustomed the Turks to long periods of inaction, during which 23,000 British and 4,000 French troops were withdrawn, the grand plan left 17,000 men to be evacuated on the final night.

Captain Freddie Guest (1875-1937) of Canford Manor, the MP for East Dorset, became aide-de-camp to Field-Marshal Sir John French, commander of the British Expeditionary Force in France. Although he could not save his boss from Lord Kitchener's wrath and the butcher's bill on the Western Front, in 1917, as Prime Minister Lloyd George's Chief Whip, Freddie was in a position to do a favour for his cousin, Winston Churchill.

Having lost his Admiralty portfolio, Winston could well have stayed out of Government indefinitely, but partly as a result of Freddie's insistence, he came back to Whitehall as Minister of Munitions.

Then – like mother, like son – Freddie Guest was caught up in a scandal following revelations that honours were being sold. He was more than just naive, as with an overturned election result in 1910, and believed the maxim of his mother, Lady Cornelia Wimborne, that everyone had their price. It never occurred to him that there could be anything wrong in such a system. He then tried to form alliances with just about anyone who had a vote in the House of Commons. Coalitions were variously suggested with Conservatives, Unionists, Asquith's breakaway Liberal faction and, failing all else, the Labour Party. When the press could no longer take this seriously, Freddie and a few friends bought the *Daily Chronicle*, to turn it into a Liberal newspaper and provide themselves with an alternative platform.

four

Patriotism plus Beacons at Bridport

DURING A PERIOD of terrible anxiety, when war and peace were hanging in the balance, uneventful life went on as normal in Bridport. Summer holiday-makers came to West Bay as usual through 1914, by train and on Cosen & Company's 229-ton paddle-steamer *Victoria* from Weymouth. To the town's newspaper reporter, John Rowson, there seemed 'no such hateful thing as war to mar and destroy the happiness which God intended for his creatures'. But when the declaration of war was made known, from the *Bridport News* office at 34 West Street, all was changed.

War against Germany was announced to the House of Commons by Sir Edward Grey, the Secretary of State for Foreign Affairs, on Tuesday 4 August 1914. The previous day he had spelt out its implications which would see the inherently peaceful people of pleasant places such as Bridport finding themselves backstage at Armageddon:

> *'The lamps are going out all over Europe; we shall not see them lit again in our lifetime.'*

The implications were not widely realised. To most in the seaboard counties the Royal Navy was as powerful and paramount as ever, although the gathering toll of slaughter and sacrifice soon brought home fearful realities to a town of nearly 6,000 people. Hundreds besieged the *Bridport News* offices for the latest news and all became bustle and excitement, for there was scarcely a British fighting ship on the sea but had a Bridport man in her crew. Many men from the town were serving in the Army, and time-expired men had passed into the Reserve. A total of 700 Bridport men would leave the town to play their part for 'King and Country'. Rowson reported the moment of call-up:

> *'Reveille rang through the town one morning at five o'clock.'*

It was a summons for men of the 1st Dorset Battery, Royal Field Artillery, to report for foreign service. They were mustered by Captain G. D. Nantes as he awaited the arrival of Major Leger Livingstone-Learmonth from Child Okeford. The Town Clerk, Charles George Nantes, prepared the formal civic goodbyes. These territorial soldiers were already inside the military net. Efforts were immediately under way to convince and cajole their peers to volunteer to join them. To Rowson, there was only one legitimate excuse for staying at home:

'Only young farmers without old fathers, who could take over from them, were exempt from going to foreign fields.'

Canon Henry Richard William Farrer, rector since 1895 and rural dean for the Bridport area, organised a special service of intercession for the first Sunday of the war, in St Mary's parish church, on 9 August 1914. He led prayers for 'divine mercy and the safety of our empire'. The service ended with the singing of 'God Save the King' and the national anthem would continue to be sung at the end of church services for the duration of the war. Canon Farrer's services became increasingly patriotic and strident. The canon was a recruiting sergeant, urging parishioners from the pulpit:

'Fight for England, home, and beauty.'

On 30 August 1914 his sermon became a lecture on the practicalities of military strategy. Reporter John Rowson recalled that Canon Farrer predicted German intentions, towards France, and the need for a substantial British Expeditionary Force when he said that 'we ought to be able to put half a million men on the continent at Ostend'. This would have blocked the enemy movement down the Channel, which was soon taking place, that enabled Germany to establish a submarine base at Zeebrugge. Canon Farrer expected everyone to do their duty:

'It is no time to think that young men may remain sitting on their office stools in the banks or in the counting houses and say they are not wanted yet. They are wanted. They are wanting now. Every young man must decide, either to his shame to stay at home, or he must answer his country's call now, at once, and say – "Here I am, use me for my country's good".'

Lieutenant-Colonel Thomas Colfox, of Coneygar and the Dorset Yeomanry, set about erecting a beacon on the East Cliff at West Bay, and Captain Alfred Douglas Pass from Wootton Fitzpaine built one on Thorncombe Beacon, on a site used in 1588 to bring warning of the Spanish Armada. Another was made at Abbotsbury, and so on east and west along the coast. At the time it was considered possible that a German raiding party might land in Lyme Bay and that their first action would be to cut telegraph and telephone wires. In such an event there would have been no means of giving prompt notice to the naval base at Portland but by these beacon fires. The great heap of 'wood and tar barrels' on East Cliff, above Bridport Harbour, was to stay in place for the duration of a war that, people said, would be 'over by Christmas'.

Instead, on the horizon off West Bay, Christmas was followed by a shock that showed the war was only just beginning – the sinking of the battleship *Formidable* – which will be the subject of the next chapter.

By this time, more than 500 men from Bridport and neighbourhood had come forward to recruiting officer Colonel Colfox and the mayor, William George Fowler, who had doubted there would ever be a war with Germany but soon led the community effort by chairing a recruitment meeting at the Town Hall. Major Joseph Gundry, from the town's netting factory, was appointed Inspector of Railway Defence in Ireland.

Volunteers were sought to 'keep vigilant observation' over local reservoirs day and night. Even the Boy Scouts – founded in Dorset in 1908 by Lieutenant-General Robert Baden-Powell 'to promote good citizenship in the rising generation' – found themselves mobilised for the war effort. They were given a major role in the task of keeping watch over the reservoirs of Bridport Waterworks. Baden-Powell encouraged their efforts by publishing his memoirs under the title *My Adventures as a Spy*.

On the coast, those with naval experience cautioned that Portland was no longer the bulwark that everyone thought, particularly after the hasty departure of most of its warships. The town's newspaper reporter, John Rowson, author of *Bridport in the Great War*, shared these fears and thought the frayed state of war nerves was justified:

> *'We were undoubtedly in very great danger at that time, and it was thought possible that an attacking force might land somewhere in Lyme Bay. So that every precaution might be taken for the saving of life and limb the War Office issued an order that on the notification of the presence of the enemy the inhabitants were at once to make their way inland. Homes were to be abandoned, not a wheel was to be left behind, nor any horses or cattle that might be turned to use by the enemy; they were to be destroyed or sent forward. This was the first thing to bring home to the minds of the people the terrible conditions of war in an invaded land. There was no panic, but so real was it that many actually collected their money and valuables to carry off with them in their flight.'*

The War Office had already commandeered the best horses in the county:

> *'In this, as in everything else, nothing matters but to win the war, and any trade inconvenience caused by the heavy drafts of horses from the neighbourhood is cheerfully borne in a spirit of patriotism. The Great Western Railway Company has but two dray horses left to do all the carting from the station yard at Bridport. Nearly all the brewery horses were taken, and farmers, carters and tradespeople generally were equally affected. Owners had to bring their horses to the Artillery Parade Ground at the bottom of St Michael's Lane where they [were] tethered in long lines to await veterinary inspection. Mounted Yeomanry gathered in the Square at Broadwindsor as their predecessors had for centuries at moments of national tension.'*

Refugees were found homes in Bridport. Forty of 'these derelicts of war' – as Rowson described them – stepped off the train on Thursday 26 November 1914. They were 'fleeing from their country homeless and destitute' after the Germans had invaded neutral Belgium in order to side-step French defences on its border with Holland. In Bridport this 'sad and dejected company' were found empty houses, included holiday accommodation and homes vacated by soldiers going to war, which were taken over and furnished. Men, women and children had fled from Antwerp, Douay and Malines with 'all that remained of their worldly belongings' in bundles, baskets, and in one case a galvanised bucket.

On their trek to the Channel ports they had survived on raw turnips. In Bridport, Sister Mary Elizabeth made the Visitation Convent in Pymore Road available as a reception centre and gave them a substantial meal. Some 40 more, already on their way, arrived in time for a morale-boosting concert, hosted by the mayor, in the Rifle Drill Hall. Thomas Hervey Beams, master of Bradpole Elementary School, organised a December delivery of a cart load of vegetables and other produce which was gathered by children from their allotment plots. Other gifts arrived from around the town and surrounding villages.

A framed portrait of King Albert of the Belgians dominated the Christmas gathering in the Town Hall. Messages were read from the Prime Minister, the Right Honourable Herbert Henry Asquith, and the novelist Sir Hall Caine who had articulated the nation's tribute to Belgian bravery. Three 'noble Belgian families' were housed in apartments in the harbourside Pier Terrace at West Bay. For her part in co-ordinating the town's Refugee Committee, the Mayoress, Mrs Cornick, was awarded the Medal of Queen Elizabeth by the King of the Belgians. The Mayor was later given King Albert's Medal, with ribbon, and the Town Clerk, Charles George Nantes, received the Golden Palms Medal. What embarrassed the town was the name of the King of Prussia public house in East Street and it was renamed the King of Belgium Hotel.

The reality of war was also being brought home to Dorset families. Albert Ernest Greenham, called up on 3 August, became Bridport's first fatality of the war on 15 October 1914. He went down with HMS *Hawke*, a cruiser with a distinctive profile of twin funnels between tall masts, when she was torpedoed by a U-boat. The first Bridport loss from the Western Front was R. G. Tite, recruited on 5 August, who joined the 1st Battalion, Dorsetshire Regiment, in France. He was killed on 22 October 1914, in the loss of 'a bump in the line' at Violaines during the retreat from Mons, when 'the enemy took the trenches at the point of the bayonet'.

Walter Cliff was lost with the battleship HMS *Good Hope* and West Bay Coastguard R. F. Buckler with HMS *Monmouth*, when the warships were torpedoed, also in the North Sea, on 1 November 1914. HMS *Bulwark* exploded on 26 November and the new cruiser HMS *Audacious* was blown up by a German mine in the Irish Sea. The loss of such 'castles of steel' – to the underhand techniques of new warfare – had a great impact on the national psyche. It became clear that Britannia was failing to rule the waves.

Solace came from far away from Europe with the sinking of four German warships in the South Atlantic, as the European war took on a global dimension. The action off the Falkland Islands on 8 December 1914 showed that the Royal Navy could still 'sweep the seas'. Submarines took another Bridport life in February 1915 when Edward William Gray was lost with a Royal Navy destroyer in the North Sea. Lionel Daubney joined him, in similar circumstances, in August 1915. The oldest enemy –

the weather – also remained active, claiming Frederick George Crabb who was washed overboard from the destroyer HMS *Midge* in the North Sea on 18 August 1915.

Canon Farrer's sermons from the pulpit of St Mary's Church became increasingly belligerent, particularly when he pointed his finger Kitchener-style and quoted from the War Lord's Guildhall speech of 9 July 1915:

> *'Tomorrow will be Monday, and my message to all of you of military age is that you must enlist in the morning. Men, materials and money are the immediate necessities. Does the call of duty find no response in you until reinforced – let us say superseded – by the call of compulsion?'*

On 31 December 1915 the extension to the railway from the town to West Bay closed to passenger traffic for the duration of hostilities. Increasing numbers of casualties led to the women of Bridport forming a Voluntary Aid Detachment of the Red Cross Society under the command of Miss C. A. Colfox. Schools and large country houses were offered for emergency hospital accommodation. More might have been achieved but for the death of Lady Williams of Bridehead, Littlebredy, who was the original vice-president of Bridport branch of the Dorset Red Cross. Her husband, Colonel Sir Robert Williams, remained Member of Parliament for West Dorset until retirement in 1922.

They had pressed the claim that Bridport was well situated for a convalescent hospital but the economics and scale of total war were such that the authorities would not cater for a location that could cater for 'only half a train'. They decided that Bridport was at the wrong end of its branch railway – lacking platform space for a full hospital train – and medical equipment earmarked for the project was packed away into the Masonic Hall in East Street.

Orderlies from Bridport served across the county and the country. The town responded enthusiastically to Queen Alexandra's appeal for needlework guilds to join the war effort. Bridport Working Party knitted and packed bandages, bedding and clothing for casualties and the dispossessed. Austen Whetham's house in South Street became a supply depot, run by Mrs C. F. S. Sanctuary from Mangerton, at Netherbury, which gathered a total of 1,850 garments and 13,500 surgical dressings.

Major William Townley Whetham of 67 Victoria Grove, the pre-war commander of the Bridport Rifles, formed a Town Guard. The determined septuagenarian found fellow old soldiers and launched an appeal for funds to buy rifles. Calling themselves the Bridport Company they later opened their ranks to younger non-military volunteers, as 'a broader civil defence corps that could respond to any emergency'. Captain J. Suttill and Second-Lieutenant F. W. Knight were its principal officers.

There were moments of hilarity. One band of coast watchers at Seatown went to sleep on the job and were put to shame by having their fish dinner stolen from under their noses. Constant rumours of U-boats surreptitiously slipping into the inhospitable shore around Lyme Regis for supplies all proved groundless but in the process wasted much police time. The only alleged traitor caught on the cliffside turned out to be a fossil collector. Similar false alarms came from the watch ships in Lyme Bay which kept an eye on the shore as well as shipping movements in the English Channel. Their sighting of someone at Eype who was signalling to U-boats in Morse code was found to be a lady 'arranging her tresses before retiring to bed, oblivious of the fact that she had not drawn the blind'.

A 'harmless cripple' attracted suspicion after making his home in the empty Coastguard Station at Burton Bradstock. One evening he was being kept under police surveillance when a military unit was alerted to something strange going on. They sealed off the coast road and arrested cyclists and pedestrians passing through the village.

Among the first catch was the police sergeant from Bridport who headed eastwards when he received a secret message that his constable from Burton Bradstock was missing. On his own initiative the man had decided to keep watch upon the disabled man in the Coastguard Station and had himself been observed hiding in the bushes. He was then watched by soldiers. When Sergeant Frank Bishop peddled towards him they closed the net. The muddle was not resolved – and the policemen and other suspects released – until two o'clock in the morning.

Ration coupons were necessary for hotel meals costing in excess of 1s. 2d. or teas for sixpence or more. For a time, white bread and full cream were taken out of rationing, and could only be supplied to children, invalids, and patients with authorisation from a doctor.

Boatmen required a permit from the district officer in Charge of Coast-Watching. That issued at Exmouth, to William Farwell of Brook Cottage, Mill Lane, Chideock, was for the operation of *Two Sisters* from the beach at Seatown:

> *'This vessel is allowed to proceed within the area sanctioned by Notice to Mariners during daylight hours only. Daylight to be considered from half-an-hour before Sunrise till half-an-hour after Sunset. If caught out by fog the vessel must return to shore at once.'*

Restrictions under the Defence of the Realm Act, 1916, included severe licensing laws, which were to stay in force for decades. The intention was to curb opportunities for drinking rather than working. Zeppelin airships brought a new fear and a blackout was imposed and enforced to lessen the chances of 'diabolical air raids on unprotected cities, towns and villages'. None took place over Dorset but suitable alarms, such as Gundry's factory hooter at Bridport, were kept in readiness, to sound a 'take cover' warning.

John Rowson remembered it as adding an extra layer of uncertainty to a growing anxiety over the human cost of stalemate in the trenches:

> *'It does not require much effort of the imagination to realise the sadness and desolation of those days, with heart-breaking news coming through week by week of loved ones killed in action, dying in hospitals, wounded, missing or prisoners of war. But the greatness of human character comes out more nobly in the hour of affliction than under normal conditions, and although the old*

light-heartedness was gone, and the smile had given place in many instances to a grief-stricken countenance, no one lost heart, and there was that quiet determination to go on unfalteringly to the end, so characteristic of the British people and so dreaded by our enemies. Old men were ready, if necessary, to take the place of their fallen sons, and continue the fight so earnestly begun, that those young lives might not have been lost in vain.'

The practice lines on Eype Down dug by the Royal Naval Division in January 1915 were taken over by the East Lancashire Regiment for their trench-training exercises.

Wartime unemployment was unknown in Bridport and District. The town's netting works and their armies of outworkers produced hemp lanyards for the Army and Navy. White lanyards for sailors to wear around their necks and plaited and twisted shoulder lanyards were delivered in millions, representing something like 300 tons in weight. Likewise there was a huge demand for tent lines and twines of all descriptions.

The Royal Navy's requirements included fishing seine-nets, in large quantities, so that warships at sea could catch fresh fish. The Air Board ordered balloon and aeroplane cordage, with one firm maintaining a continuous supply of six tons per week. In 1917 the idea of camouflage netting was widely adopted, not only for hiding war material and gun emplacements in France, but for generally disguising the movements of troops. Netting was being made in Bridport in huge quantities, both by machine and by hand, for all kinds of uses.

Because of the big demand for women workers on the land, as an alternative form of National Service, the War Office told net-workers that they were already engaged in the war effort. Manufacturers were instructed to copy this notice to all outworkers and braiders in the district:

'It is hoped to reassure them that in braiding these particular nets they are making their highest possible contribution to the war effort. Even such mundane products as potato nets and pea nets have a military application, being used by our troops for boiling these vegetables.'

Down on East Beach, the horses and carts of Norman Good and Phillips & Son continued to gather sand and shingle for the building of fortifications and other war works. Regular goods trains left the sidings at West Bay Station. One railwayman talked in the town of 'coals to Newcastle' after hearing that a consignment was being shipped to Egypt. Others believed the remark was the purchasing officer's way of telling him to refrain from asking questions in wartime.

One of the few happy stories from the Western Front was that a maid servant at Bridport had put her name and address inside one of the pairs of socks she had knitted for the troops. They were amongst the bundles sent to the battery commanded by Major (later Sir) Philip Colfox (1888-1966). The soldier who got them wrote to her full of gratitude and from this a correspondence developed. On his first leave, he came to Bridport, proposed to the girl, and was accepted. By the time Major Colfox told the story, they were married, 'with a bright and happy prospect in front of them'.

five

The 'Formidable' Tragedy

DORSET'S GREAT NAVAL TRAGEDY of the Great War took place in Lyme Bay at 02.20 hours on New Year's Day in 1915. The 15,000-ton battleship HMS *Formidable*, sailing last in line with the 5th Battle Squadron from Portland, was torpedoed 20 miles east of Start Point. German submarine *UB-24* was responsible, with two torpedoes from close range, but itself only narrowly survived, having grazed the warship's heaving keel.

Then the warship settled into a stable state, enabling an orderly evacuation, but at 04.39 she slipped under quite suddenly. Deteriorating weather had hampered the rescue operation. Of the crew of 780, only 233 survived. Some were in the ship's own cutter which struggled for 20 hours to reach land at Lyme Regis. The Brixham trawler *Provident* made heroic efforts to help, as did the escort cruisers HMS *Topaz* and *Diamond*, which together brought a total of 80 sailors to Portland Harbour. For the remaining 547 officers and men the sea became their grave.

HMS Formidable *sailing with the 5th Battle Squadron.*

The ship's dog, an old terrier named Bruce, was also lost. He was last seen standing on duty beside his master, Captain Loxley, who remained with Commander Ballard on the bridge. Revd G. Brooke Robinson, former curate of Burton Bradstock and a

HMS Diamond *arrives in Port-land on 1 January 1915 with survivors from the* Formidable.

prominent member of West Bay Swimming Club, who was chaplain on board, also went down with the ship.

There were 50 men aboard the ship's boat washed up at Lyme. Nine of them were dead or dying. Others had expired during the voyage, from injuries and exposure, and their bodies had been pushed overboard. At Lyme the press found their second 'Man's best friend' story.

Survivors' defiant message – 'HMS Formidable. *Are We Downhearted? 1st Jan 1915' - photographed at Portland by Captain G. C. C. Crookshank.*

John Cowen had been left for dead on the floor of the Pilot Boat Inn in Broad Street. During the night, however, the landlord's cross-breed collie started licking his face and

hands. Charles Atkins drew attention to the dog's agitation and a groan was heard to come from the body. From the jaws of disaster the media had their miracle to report:

> *'Immediately willing hands completed the work the dog had started and in a short time Cowen sat up. Since then the dog and Cowen have been insepa-rable, and as Cowen is not yet allowed out, he and the dog spend most of the time before the kitchen fire cultivating the acquaintance so curiously begun.'*

On the other end of the scale, for warships, the 162-ton HMT *Quail III* – the initials standing for His Majesty's Trawler – was run over and sunk by an unidentified vessel off Portland Bill on 23 June 1915. The Admiralty designated Portland Harbour as a War Anchorage and Trawler Station and placed it in control of English Channel sea-area XIII, which became known as Portland Command Area.

The sea off Dorset became the new front line as Admiral Henning von Holtzendorff turned his force of 130 U-boats – only 60 of which were at sea at any one time – into a decisive weapon. By April 1917 they were not only responsible for sinking a total of 860,000 tons of shipping but had forced hundreds of neutral merchantmen to stay in port, their crews refusing orders to sail. Oil tankers were a particularly attractive and east target, with the result that the Royal Navy's fuel supplies from Hampton Roads in the United States were reduced to such low levels that British battleships of the Grand Fleet were allowed to sail at full speed only in an emergency.

six

Bovington and Lulworth Tanks

A FOURTH DORSET CONTRIBUTION to the war that was directly due to an intervention by Winston Churchill was the arrival in Bovington and Lulworth of the world's first tanks. The county also saw the construction of the first anti-tank trenches at Gallows Hill on heathland above Bere Regis. War Office representatives had declined to promote the idea of Lieutenant-Colonel (Sir) Ernest Swinton, who had published *The Defence of Duffer's Drift* under the pseudonym 'Backsight Forethought', for an armed and armoured motorised vehicle moving on tracks. Swinton was serving his country as a war correspondent rather than a soldier. His project was adopted by Churchill as First Lord of the Admiralty.

Tank humour.

The Naval Landships Committee was formed on 20 February 1915 under the chairmanship of (Sir) Eustace Tennyson d'Eyncourt. The first special demonstration, starring a Killen-Stuart tractor, impressed both officers and politicians. Improvisations were courtesy Lieutenant W. W. G. Wilson and (Sir) William Tritton whose William Foster engineering company made the 'Centipede' tracked vehicles. The two discussed their ideas in the White Hart Hotel at Lincoln.

Fosters won the contract for the prototype 'Tritton' with a 105-horsepower 6-cylinder Daimler engine and tail-wheels for improved steering and stability. It was to move at walking speed. King George V watched the machine go through its trials on Thetford Heath, Norfolk. Its competition was a mock-up 'Wilson' which differed in having all-around perimeter tracks as these offered a better chance of spanning an 8-feet trench and mounting a 4.5-feet parapet. Swinton insisted that the armour had to withstand a 'reversed' bullet fired from 30 feet (reversing the bullet to the blunt end enhanced its armoured-piercing capability). The armament was to be two Hotchkiss 6-pounder guns and four machine-guns.

Wilson's design won through. The guns were balanced in large sponsons, on each side of a 26.5-feet long vehicle, 8-feet high and weighing 28 tons. 'Mother's' first outing was on 16 January 1916 and Lord Salisbury gave approval for a trial in Hatfield Park on 2 February. It was at this stage that a sensible name was needed to explain away a large object behind tarpaulins on a flat-bed railway wagon without attracting attention. Something with watery associations would be appropriate for what was still a naval project. Swinton discussed the possibilities with Lieutenant-Colonel W. Dalby Jones.

'Tank' was chosen after 'cistern' and 'container' were rejected. Lord Kitchener reserved his judgement on its potential effectiveness, but the King remained enthusiastic, and was taken for a ride on 8 February. To Major-General John Fuller, who had been told to expect something ugly, it was something else:

> '... *not a monster, but a very graceful machine, with beautiful lines, lozenge-shaped, but with two clumsy-looking wheels behind it.*'

He was the first to liken it to 'an armoured mechanical horse'. This was the tank that then came to Dorset before it went to war.

Two versions of Wilson's Mark I prototype were produced, with the 'Male' having 6-pounder guns on each side and the 'Female' mounting two Vickers' machine-guns in each sponson. Swinton persuaded the War Office to increase the initial request from the British Expeditionary Force in France (for 40 tanks for France) to an order for 200 vehicles (25 from Foster's and 175 from the Metropolitan Carriage and Wagon Company). Soon another 50 were on order.

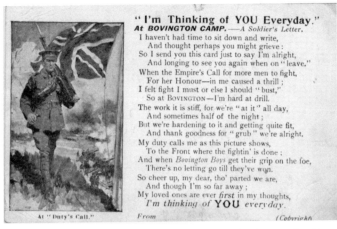

'Dear Mother' postcard to Mrs James in Thame, Oxfordshire, 1915.

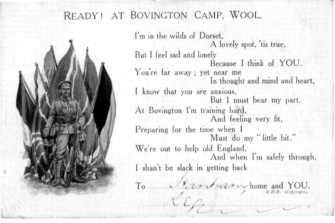

'Dear Mother' postcard to Mrs K. Sweet at Hanham, Bristol, in May 1916.

Bovington Camp and the road to Clouds Hill.

Trench-crossing demonstration at Bovington.

Left: *Tank Park mechanics at Bovington distracted by something smaller.*

Right: *That sinking feeling in Dorset's boggy heathland.*

Tank D11, immobilised on the Western Front, September 1916.

General Swinton was appointed Commander-in-Chief of the nascent Tank Detachment with Lieutenant-Colonel (Sir) Hugh Elles, from the Royal Engineers, as its Field Commander in France. The War Office then feared that the job descriptions would compromise the element of secrecy that surrounded the new weapon. So the unit was re-named the Heavy Branch, Machine-Gun Corps (and did not become the Tank Corps until 28 July 1917, and the Royal Tank Corps by royal warrant on 18 October 1923). Swinton was given an establishment of 184 officers and 1,610 other ranks, who were to be found by the Machine-Gun Corps at its Belton House base near Grantham, Lincolnshire. They gathered as a unit at Canada Farm, Elvedon, near Thetford.

British tank crossing a German trench.

The tanks were to be moved south, firstly to Siberia Farm, Bisley Camp, Surrey, and then to a secret location amid miles of desolate Wessex heathland. Colonel Swinton, delighted with the capabilities of the modified version christened *Little Willie*, assumed command of the Tank Detachment on 16 February 1916.

Novelist and poet Thomas Hardy's native heath between Wool and Bere Regis was chosen for the battle-training area before the machines were shipped to the Western Front. Swinton clinched the move to Dorset within 24 hours of being asked to find an alternative to Elvedon:

> *'The wooded country around Bovington is particularly adapted to the training of tank battalions, the rolling downs, the woods and the small streets being very similar to and as equally deserted as the battlefields of France.'*

A thousand acres had been bought for military training, from Mrs Louisa Mary Featherstonhaugh Frampton of Moreton House, for £4,300 in 1899. The land was extended with the acquisition from Lieutenant-Colonel Edmund Mansel-Pleydell of 290 acres of Chamberlayne's Heath, in 1907, followed by a further 16 acres in 1910.

Mishap beside Wool Bridge.

The men were based in a tented and hutted camp beside Bovington Farm. An extensive network of practice trenches was dug across Bere Heath, Higher Hyde Heath and Stoke Heath. Most represented the German lines that were to be attacked. they were faced on the Bovington side by the British defences – Roberts Trench and Gordon Trench, approached from Piccadilly, Regent Street and Bond Street from Lovers Valley, Blighty Valley and Happy Valley respectively. Forward of the enemy's main Kaiser Line were Boar's Head, Mad Point and Wunder Work with the Hohenzollern Redoubt on the right flank.

Tank railway beside the River Frome.

The next strong-points were Big Willie, Little Willie and Fritz Redoubt with Three Sisters Redoubt blocking the western approach to Gallows hill and Stuff Redoubt, Kluck Redoubt and Schweben Redoubt. Hulke Trench, Willoughby Trench, Hankey Trench, Woods Trench and Colson Trench weaved up the slope from the Ladies' lookout on South Heath to Fort Anley on the south-west side of Gallows Hill. That was the ultimate strong-point, the Gallows Redoubt. Its rearguard were the Potsdam and Berlin Lines on Warren Heath and forward of the Black Castle pinewoods.

On chalk hills to the south, St Andrew's Farm, inland from Bindon Hill at West Lulworth, was chosen for live-firing gunnery practice. Nelson Thomson, a Purbeck quarryman who retired to Acton at Langton Matravers, remembered the arrival of the first tanks, and looked back to 1916, when he talked to me in 1971. He was a young shepherd for Alan Budden at Burngate Farm, the next farm up the slope from St Andrew's:

> *'When they used to bring the tanks over from Bovington they used to shut us behind screens of hurdles or take us away so that we couldn't see them. They*

The Tank Park at Bovington.

put on Army control all along the roads and if anybody was within sight they used to put them off. It didn't make any difference, because, when we were at Lulworth, the tanks was going along the road – and we was watching them.

'What I used to have to do was to take the sheep down on to the range from five o'clock to nine o'clock in the morning and then they started firing and I had to bring them back. Then at two o'clock I'd bring them down, some days, from two to three o'clock and then back again. And then from six o'clock to eight o'clock in the evening. One time there I can remember a military policeman came out and started chasing me. I had troops and sheep and everything all mixed up together out of the square, opposite from where their tank was.

'Where Lulworth Camp started it was all tents. They were sleeping under canvas. I can remember when the Post Office at Lulworth got hit with a shell. I don't know whether it was 1916 but there was an awful disturbance about it. Two shells went adrift somewhere – they said ricocheted – and the Post Office and one of the houses got hit. The shells came from the tanks on the tank range at Lulworth.'

Taking over St Andrew's Farm for what became Lulworth Camp was a secret operation. Landowner Charles Joseph Weld-Blundell of Lulworth Castle received prior notification but no one passed this on to the farming tenants. Nelson Thomas recalled that they were only given a few hours to leave, and it was not until midnight that they departed, down the road to stay with Mr Ford at Coombe Keynes.

Of the first 100 tanks to reach France, 49 went into action on 15 September 1916. It was D-Company of the Heavy Branch, Machine-Gun Corps that achieved the moment of historical significance, which was witnessed from an aeroplane:

Tank gunnery camp at Lulworth.

'Creme de Menthe [a tank] is walking up the street of Flers with the British Army cheering behind.'

Brigadier-General Frederick Gore Anley (1864-1936), who had led the 12th Infantry Brigade at the battles of Marne, the Aisne and Ypres, was brought home from the Western Front to take charge of the newly established Tank Training Centre at Bovington Camp on 20 October 1916. The 7th (Depot) Battalion, Dorsetshire Regiment, provided support facilities, under Lieutenant-Colonel F. P. Smyly. E, F, G, H and I battalions of the Heavy Branch were each provided with 72 tanks. The eastern parade ground, west of the Clouds Hill road at the north end of the camp, became a Tank Park with a growing number of buildings. It eventually comprised a repair shed, ten repair bays, workshops and the mechanical school. The five Battalion Tank Parks were a little further along the road, on the opposite side.

The initiative and potential that the tank brought to the science of warfare was poorly handled by the High Command. It was not until 19 August 1917 that the Tank Corps could celebrate an outstanding success. The decision was taken to knock out a string of German pill-boxes at St Julien. Their walls were of reinforced concrete, a metre thick, which were anticipated to cost a thousand British casualties. Instead, in a departure from usual practice, the tanks advanced from the British line without any preliminary bombardment. Infantry followed under a smoke screen. The strongpoints were taken with only two British deaths.

On 20 November 1917, Brigadier-General Elles – flying the new Tank Corps banner from an ash wand – led a massed force of 350 tanks in *Hilda*. They smashed through every line of trenches in the German front for the first time since the stalemate of trench warfare. It had been estimated that such a breakthrough would take five months and require a total of £20 million of ammunition. As a result, no infantry had been allocated to support and consolidate the offensive, which became another wasted opportunity.

There followed a great British cover-up. In this the War Office had more talent than they ever showed for fighting. They excelled themselves and invented a German hero who had halted the advance. Never before had the British press been allowed to admit that there were any brave Germans. Yet here they were issued with the story of a mythical man:

> *'I came to a German field battery, every gun out of action except one. By this was lying a single German officer, quite dead. In front of him were five tanks which he had evidently succeeded in knocking out single-handed with his gun. A brave man.'*

It was a story that was put forward by reactionaries for the rest of the war, as a reason for abandoning the tank building programme but the tank was not its own justification. By the end of the war the Germans had their own tanks and the British line was broken wherever they attacked. The French also had their tanks though Fuller was unimpressed by 'a kind of kitchen range on tracks, unblushingly useless'. British tanks won the decisive battle of the First World War on 8 August 1918 when they tore a gap 11 miles wide through the German lines. Kaiser Wilhelm II remarked that evening:

> *'It is very strange that our men cannot get used to tanks.'*

A German historian credited the Allied victory to 'General Tank'. General Sir Douglas Haig, the British Commander-in-Chief, concurred in praising the tank for bringing about the Armistice:

> *'Since the opening of our offensive on 8 August tanks have been employed in every battle and the importance of the part played by them in breaking the resistance of German infantry can scarcely be exaggerated.'*

In its two years in the field, the Tank Corps led by General Elles had suffered losses of 879 dead, 935 missing, and 5,302 wounded. They won four Victoria Cross citations for valour in the face of the enemy. The first went to Captain Clement Robertson who

Squadron of tanks below Bindon Hill, Lulworth.

led his tanks of A-Battalion on foot, in order to navigate them through almost impossible terrain beside Polygon Wood, Reutel. He 'deliberately sacrificed his life to make certain of the success of his tanks' in the third Battle of Ypres on 4 October 1917.

Captain Richard William Leslie Wain was awarded the second VC. While seriously wounded, he left the safety of his tank to storm a German strong-point and take half its garrison prisoner, near Marcoing in the Hindenburg Support Line on 20 November 1917.

Lieutenant Cecil Howard Sewell of the 3rd Battalion won the third VC, for saving the life of other wounded, while injured himself, and giving his life in the process, near Fremicourt on 29 April 1918. His light Whippet tank, named *Caesar*, is now in the Tank Museum at Bovington.

Lieutenant-Colonel Richard Annersley West received the fourth VC, also posthumously, for the double actions of Courcelles on 21 August and Vaulx-Vracourt, on 2 September 1918, where he rallied his men in the face of certain death from machine-gun fire.

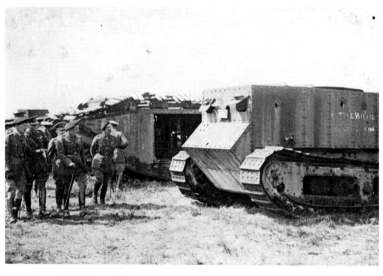

King George V (with walking stick) and Little Willie in post-war retirement at Bovington.

In Dorset, the coach company that became Shamrock & Rambler provided the Army with a charabanc. Rambler No. 4 (registration number EL 1250) ran a shuttle service between Lulworth and Bournemouth, with stops at Wareham and Poole en route. For an afternoon and evening out 'the return fare to Town was two shillings which was docked from our pay'. Departure, from the Guard Room beside the west gate on Lulworth Camp, was at 14.00 hours. The return, from The Square in Bournemouth, was at 23.00, passing through Poole at midnight.

After the war, hundreds of tanks – mostly brought back from France – accumulated in the Tank Park between Bovington Camp and Clouds Hill. Bovington, the base for the 1st (Depot) Battalion of the Tank Corps, mushroomed into a garrison of wooden huts and workshops. From 1919 to 1928 it had its own railway line, from a siding at Wool Station, which crossed the Frome at a concrete and steel slab-bridge downstream from historic Wool Bridge.

Rudyard Kipling came up with the idea for a Tank Museum in 1923 but the Great War collection was taken out into the countryside for stationery pill-boxes in 1940 and many eventually went for scrap. Just one Mark-1 survivor was left for the centrepiece of a recreation of the trenches that was opened in Bovington on 11 November 1998 to mark the 80th anniversary of the Armistice. It should have been opened by 104-year-old veteran Captain Norman Edwards but he was too frail to attend.

seven

First Flying VC

A DORSET HERO won for the Royal Flying Corps – and therefore the emergent Royal Air Force – the first Victoria Cross to be awarded for aerial warfare. The recipient of Britain's highest honour 'For Valour' in the face of the enemy was awarded for a suicidal bombing mission against a key bridge over the River Lys, beside a railway junction at Courtrai, Belgium, through which the Germans were bringing reinforcements to the Western Front. Forces were gathering in Ghent and heading for the Ypres salient. The attack took place on 26 April 1915 and succeeded in stopping reserves from reaching the front line at a crucial time in the second Battle of Ypres where the Allies were recoiling from the first-ever German gas attack.

Second-Lieutenant William Barnard Rhodes-Moorhouse (1887-1915) of the Special Reserve Flying Corps, from Parnham House at Beaminster, was flying a Farnborough-designed Bleriot-Experimental BE2b (No. 687) of 2 Squadron. The attacks on the railway, also at Roubaix and Tourcoing, were spearheaded by 7 and 8 Squadrons but four reconnaissance aircraft from 2 Squadron were tasked to join the operation.

Rhodes-Moorhouse in his Royal Flying Corps uniform.

Rhodes-Moorhouse took off from Merville at 15.05 hours, carrying a single 100-lb bomb, and headed for Courtrai. As he descended to 300 feet, to drop the bomb on the tracks, he came under a barrage of small-arms fire upwards from troops on the ground and sideways from a machine-gun mounted in the belfry of the nearby church.

Though critically wounded through the thigh and abdomen, losing considerable quantities of blood, and slipping almost into unconsciousness, Rhodes-Moorhouse succeeded in returning the BE2b to Merville. Additional wounds, to his hand and stomach, were sustained in the process as the damaged aircraft lost height over the trenches. He landed at 16.15 and insisted on writing his report on the action before leaving for the hospital. Ground-crew counted a total of 95 bullet and shrapnel holes in the airframe. He told the chaplain:

'I'm not a brave man but I have tried to do my duty.'

He died at 14.25 the following day. Such was the admiration of his commanding officer, Maurice Blake, that he implemented William's request that his body should be shipped home to Dorset for burial – itself a rare honour as it was a wish denied to almost all the other dead heroes. The *Daily Mail* was duly impressed:

> *'Such endurance is enough to make us ashamed of ever again complaining of any pain whatever. He was one of those who have never 'done their bit' till they have done the impossible.'*

BE2b aircraft as used by Rhodes-Moorhouse to bomb Courtrai.

In a letter of condolence to Linda Rhodes-Moorhouse, Squadron Leader William Sholto Douglas expressed the sentiment that William's action was worthy of the highest decoration, but avoided promising that it would be awarded:

> *'I do hope that such courage will be recognised with a DSO* [Distinguished Service Order] *although we all think a VC would be none too great a reward for such pluck and endurance.'*

The Victoria Cross was duly gazetted on 22 May. In Dorset, the inscription on his grave, in a railed burial plot overlooking Parnham House and Beaminster, reads:

> *'William Barnard Rhodes-Moorhouse, VC, RFC. Died April 27th 1915 at Merville, France, from wounds received in bombing Courtrai, aged 27 years. In sacred loving memory. Per ardua ad astra.'*

The Rhodes-Moorhouse graves at Parnham.

It glosses over the superlative. He had provided 'those magnificent men in their flying machines' with their first Victoria Cross.

William has another claim to fame – in the carefree days of pre-war aviation he had been the first to fly through the arches of the Golden Gate Bridge at San Francisco. He is also in the record books for being the first airman to fly passengers across the English Channel. That was during his honeymoon. The passengers were his bride, Linda, and a friend who he picked up in Douai. They crossed the Channel from Boulogne to

Rhodes-Moorhouse owned Parnham House.

Dungeness and landed at Bethersden, Kent, on 4 August 1912. There the Breguet tractor-biplane had to make a forced-landing, in poor visibility, though the pilot and passengers were unhurt.

Parnham House had been bought by William's Maori mother in 1913. In Dorset he left a widow and a baby son, William Henry Rhodes-Moorhouse (1914-40) who would follow his father's example in the next war and win a Distinguished Flying Cross for 601 (County of London) Squadron in the Battle of Britain. At its climax, on 6 September 1940, his Hurricane was shot down near Tonbridge, Kent. His ashes were returned to the Parnham plot. Linda Rhodes-Moorhouse had lost both her husband and her son at the same age and from the same cause.

Sotheby's sold William's Victoria Cross in 1990 for a record £125,000. It was acquired by Michael Ashcroft and presented to the trust he established to care for his collection of medals. The story features in Lord Ashcroft's book *Victoria Cross Heroes*. An RAF VC10 transport aircraft of 10 Squadron (airframe number XV108) was named *William Rhodes Moorhouse VC*.

eight

Louis Strange's Remarkable Air War

Dorset's veteran flyer, Louis Strange, flew through both world wars.

FOR LONGEVITY IN THE AIR, also stretching through the entirety of the Second World War, no one was to match the record of Louis Arbon Strange (1891-1966). He was born at Keynston Mill, beside the River Stour at Tarrant Crawford, moved to Almer, Sturminster Marshall, and in later life established a private airfield on his own farm at Worth Matravers.

He joined the Queen's Own Dorsetshire Yeomanry and threw himself into its outdoor activities, crediting such 'fun and games' with enabling his amazing series of survival feats in novel three-dimensional warfare. It was the Bournemouth Flying Display, at Southbourne in July 1910, that introduced him to international aviators. There the Honourable Charles Rolls became the first Briton to be killed during powered flight.

For Louis Strange his first flight was in 1911, over Dorset with Hendon instructor Lewis Turner, who came from Sturminster Newton. Louis foresaw the value of aerial reconnaissance but found the military was full of doubters. During lively banter at a cavalry camp, in May 1913, Louis bet that in a year he would learn to fly and prove it by buzzing over their heads. He went to Hendon and trained on a 35-horsepower Caudron tractor biplane. On 5 August 1913, after three weeks in London and four hours in the air, he was awarded certificate No. 575 by the Royal Aero Club.

He immediately applied for a commission in the Royal Flying Corps (RFC). Then pioneer aviator Claude Grahame-White talent-spotted Louis Strange as a potential demonstrator of his Box-Kite biplanes. Soon Louis was performing in displays and taking up passengers for a spin. He made flights in every available machine including the Henri Farman and Morane biplanes and the innovative Bleriot monoplane. In September 1913 he won a cross-country race from Hendon to Mill Hill and back. During October he instructed 22 pupils and took up 15 passengers.

By now he was one of the famous Hendon flyers and already had a reputation for daring-do when, on 4 April 1914, his picture appeared in *Flight* as one of 'the five pilots who, at Hendon Aerodrome, each for the first time looped the loop on Wednesday last week'. He was also feted as the 'cross-country flyer to watch' in the *Daily Mail* air-race to Manchester and back, in an 80-horsepower Bleriot X1-2 on 20 June 1914. His 'sleek, racy-looking monoplane' Louis was the first to arrive at Trafford Park. Alderman (Sir) Daniel M'Cabe, the Lord Mayor of Manchester, clambered on to the machine to shake his hand, but in the process broke the fuselage bracing wires and eliminated Louis from the race.

The previous month, at the War Office, Major (Sir) Sefton Brancker had approved Louis Strange's application to join the RFC. He was told to report for training to Central Flying School at Upavon, Wiltshire. Having won prizes for accuracy in flour-bombing, he was disappointed to be told that ground-support reconnaissance was the only conceivable military role for an aircraft, and then to hear of General Sir Douglas Haig's pronouncement at Aldershot in July:

> *'I hope none of you gentlemen is so foolish to think that aeroplanes will be usefully employed for reconnaissance in the air. There is only one way for a commander to get information by reconnaissance and that is by the use of cavalry.'*

Louis Strange in a sketch by war artist Captain Cuthbert Orde.

Not everyone in the War Office was a dinosaur or a donkey. With mobilisation, Lieutenant Louis Strange was ordered to report to RFC headquarters at Farnborough and went from there to Gosport, to join No. 5 Squadron at Fort Grange. A total of four operational squadrons, all with unarmed scout-planes, were being prepared to join the British Expeditionary Force. Thirty-seven pilots were ordered to gather at Dover and fly to France, to Amiens, on 14 August 1914.

Carrying a mechanic and – uniquely – a Lewis gun, Louis Strange flew in a Henri Farman F-20 which had to struggle up-Channel against the wind. The aeroplane suffered a broken longeron on bouncing across a ditch above Dover Castle. The mechanic was arrested for having downed a bottle of scotch during the two-hour flight:

> *'I did not leave the white cliffs of Old England until the disgracefully late hour of noon on Sunday, August 16th.'*

One of the aircraft stalled, near Amiens, killing its pilot and mechanic. The RFC established itself at Maubeuge. On 22 August, Strange scrambled his Farman after a German Taube trespassed over the airfield. With Lieutenant Penn Gaskell, he set off after the intruder, as Trevor Henshaw records in *The Sky Their Battlefield*:

> *'In Strange's typical indefatigable way, he had unofficially mounted a Lewis gun to his aircraft and his observer managed to fire it off at the fast escaping enemy machine. The gun also painfully diminished the aircraft's performance and it was ordered to be removed, so that next time they took a rifle.'*

Later that day the squadron lost Second-Lieutenant V. E. Waterfall and Lieutenant C. G. Bayly, in an Avro 504, over Belgium. The following day the retreat from Mons became a rout and the RFC withdrew in quick succession to Le Cateau, St Quentin, La Fere, Senlis and Juilly. Crucially, Strange was first to report a change of direction by the German First Army which put it on course for British and French counter-attacks. Sir John French credited the RFC for providing the decisive intelligence which led to the Germans being forced back to the River Aisne where mobility gave way to stagnation. Trench warfare had begun.

The Royal Flying Corps after flying to France.

On 28 August, Strange and Penn Gaskell made three petrol bombs and dropped them that afternoon, on a German transport column near St Quentin. Two missed but the third set fire to two lorries. In October, Strange swapped his Farman for an Avro 504 which, with a 80-horsepower Gnome rotary engine, which had the power to cope with providing a proper mount for the Lewis gun. Taking off from Bailleul on 22 November, with Lieutenant Small handling the machine-gun, they intercepted a German Aviatik at 7,000 feet over Armentieres. After a hairy exchange of fire, in which Freddy Small was wounded, the Aviatik plunged towards the ground with Strange in hot pursuit. He forced it down into a hedge behind the British front line.

Strange enjoyed 'three good days hunting' in Dorset, on leave in December, but was back in France for Christmas Day, 1914, when he 'bombed' the German airfield at Lille with a football. In 1915 he was sent to Paris to evaluate Aviation Militaire's new Voisin, provided with one of the first reconnaissance cameras, and as Captain Louis Strange promoted to Flight Commander of No. 6 Squadron. That meant flying a BE2c (without his beloved Lewis gun) from Poperinghe where a battle was being planned for Neuve Chappelle.

They call us THE EYES OF THE ARMY —
for we scout for the foe far and wide,
And with all Information worth having
We keep the powers fully supplied —
There are Corps who bear much longer records
For brave deeds, yet History will find
That in the great fight
for the cause of the right,
OUR AIRMEN were not FAR BEHIND.

FROM ONE OF THE R.F.C.

'Fumbs up there's something doing' was the message home on this card.

Louis Strange was tasked to take part in 'a good show at last' and sent to drop three 35-pound bombs on the railway junction at Courtrai on 10 March 1915. He descended into rifle fire but 'silenced sentry at station with a grenade' and scored direct hits on two steam trains. Seventy-five Germans were killed or injured and the line was blocked for three days. He was awarded the Military Cross for the first attack on the very place that would bring fellow Dorsetman William Rhodes-Moorhouse the RFC's first Victoria Cross [see chapter 7].

On 22 April 1915, Louis Strange and his observer, Lieutenant Hawkins, were the first to spot clouds of yellowish-green smoke drifting westwards from the German lines. They headed back to Poperinghe and personally reported to General (Sir) Herbert Plumer, at the headquarters of the 5th Army Corps, with news that poison gas was being used to open the second Battle of Ypres.

LOUIS STRANGE'S REMARKABLE AIR WAR

Strange and Lieutenant Awcock, with a rifle, shot down an Aviatik that had been pestering them and watched it spin down into Houthulst Forest. Strange's next death-defying drama took place over Polygon Wood, Menin, on 10 May 1915 when he fell out of a Martinsyde SI Scout while trying to free a jammed ammunition drum at 8,000 feet. He hung on to the airframe during an upside-down spiral of several thousand feet before hauling himself back to the controls 'within seconds of disaster' to quote the cartoon account in the magazine *Top Spot*.

Then the excitement was brought to a halt. On 2 August, Strange was summoned by his commanding officer, Gordon Shepherd, and told that as he was the only remaining flyer of the 37 pilots who had flown to France a year before, he was being posted back to England. That saw him being appointed Flight Commander of No. 12 Squadron at Netheravon. He was able to fly a BE2c down to Barn Field at Spetisbury. Soon, however, his aircraft were ready for combat and in September he took them from Hawkinge, Kent, to St Omer.

Risky business – a German airman's grave.

Strange then took charge of a Bristol Scout but just as he was fitting it with a Lewis gun, Major-General Hugh Trenchard – Commandant of the Central Flying School – made an inspection, and was annoyed to find that the flyer was back in France. He ordered him to return, and for clarity repeated the order:

'Go home at once, Strange, in that machine, now.'

This time it was Gosport and Farnborough, to form No. 23 Squadron, and have it operational by the end of the year. He was particularly adept at training night pilots – required in England to combat Zeppelin airship bombing raids – and was promoted to Major Strange to coincide with his marriage to pre-war girl friend Marjorie. Nature then intervened and it was from a bed at Cosham Military Hospital, recovering from a botched operation for appendicitis, that he watched the FE-2bs of 23 Squadron leave for France in January 1916.

His next task was to run the Machine Gun School at Hythe, on Southampton Water, which enabled him to devise 'the Strange gun mounting' for attaching automatic weapons to an aircraft fuselage. Under his tutelage, the establishment became the No. 1 School of Air Gunnery. He was then promoted to Lieutenant-Colonel Strange to form No. 2 School at Turnberry, near Girvan, Ayrshire, and a third school at Loch Doon.

In April 1917 he was appointed Assistant Commandant of the Central Flying School at Upavon. By then the German Fokkers – respected by all as the war's best fighter – were taking a constant toll and there was an endless demand for replacement pilots. In June 1917, Strange returned to France to see how techniques had evolved, and flew a Nieuport Scout on combat patrols with No. 60 Squadron. As a result, on returning to Upavon, he revised induction schedules and introduced on-board instructors, with dual-controls. This was achieved by stripping Sopwith Camel trainers of unnecessary weight and then making similar adaptations to the SE-5.

When the Royal Flying Corps merged with the Royal Naval Air Service to form the

'Bristol Fighter strafing a Hun aerodrome'.

Royal Air Force, on 1 April 1918, Louis Strange was posted north to command No. 23 (Training) Wing. He flew from Waddington to Cranwell, Lincolnshire, to show King George V and Queen Mary around the hangars and airship sheds but was prevented from landing by fog. Having made a forced-landing in a field, three miles away, he walked across country to the base.

On 26 June 1918 he returned to the Western Front, at 24 hours notice, to command the new 80th Wing of X Brigade under General Ludlow Hewitt. They forged a tactical formation with the prime objective of attacking German aircraft on their aerodromes. This reached its climax on 30 October, which turned into the heaviest single day of air fighting in the Great War. Enemy air activity was reported from Rebaix, north of Ath, and it was decided to send the entire 80th Wing there. The 62 aircraft were led by Lieutenant-Colonel Strange in his personal Sopwith Camel (number D1943). Bombers of No 2 (Australian Flying Corps), 54 and 103 Squadrons were escorted by fighters of No. 4 (AFC) and 88 Squadrons. Three hangars were set on fire and nine German fighters were claimed in the air. There were only a couple of losses. On their return the wing machine-gunned troop columns on the roads.

Louis's younger brother, Captain G. J. 'Ben' Strange of 40 Squadron, failed to return to Bryas from the dawn patrol on 24 September 1918 as the Allies prepared to attack the Hindenburg Line. His SE-5 had gone down in flames after shooting down a German fighter. Louis recorded in his log:

'Poor old Ben missing. Must hope for the best, but feel there's no chance. Cannot describe my feelings for Mother and Father.'

The fun had gone out of flying and feelings of revenge took its place. The citation for Louis Strange's Distinguished Service Order records an action on 30 October when:

'... he accompanied one of these raids against an aerodrome; watching the work of his machines, he waited until they had finished then dropped his bombs from 100 feet altitude on hangars that were undamaged, then attacked troops and transport in the vicinity of the aerodrome. Whilst thus engaged he saw eight Fokkers flying above him; at once he climbed and attacked them single handed: having driven one down out of control he was fiercely engaged by the other seven, but he maintained the combat until rescued by a patrol of our scouts.'

News of the Armistice was brought to him at 02.00 hours, French time, on 11 November 1918 with the order:

'Hostilities will cease at 11.00 today.'

Strange contemplated heading off at dawn with a few final bombs, but found someone else had 'borrowed' his Sopwith Camel. Strange expresses disappointment in his auto-biography, *Recollections of an Airman* (1933). Peter Hearn rounds off this chapter in *Flying Rebel – the story of Louis Strange* (1994):

> *'The following morning, sucking in draughts of cold air at 2,000 feet to clear his head of the previous night's celebrations, Lieutenant-Colonel Louis Strange, DSO, MC, DFC and mentioned three times in despatches, flew his battle-scarred Camel to England, there to hold his two-month-old son Brian for the first time.'*

nine

Queen's Own Dorset Yeomanry

THE VOLUNTEER CORPS of Dorset Rangers was founded in 1792, when the Prussians marched on Revolutionary France, as a territorial militia to prepare for 'actual invasion' and 'the suppression of riots and tumults'. After the Napoleonic Wars its keener members kept their skills sharp with foxhunting. By 1809, it was known as 'Dorset Yeomanry' and had been reviewed by the Duke of Cambridge, Prime Minister William Pitt and the Prince Regent. In 1834, the Duchess of Kent allowed Princess Victoria's name to be attached to the regiment, so that with her accession in 1837 it became the Queen's Own Dorset Yeomanry (QODY).

Peacetime summer camp of the QODY at Blandford.

Horse muster in the square at Broadwindsor on 5 August 1914.

Its principal Victorian distinction was to win the Lloyd Lindsay Cup for rifle-shooting, at Wimbledon, in 1876 and 1877, followed by a succession of prizes at the Royal military Tournament, Islington, between 1881 and 1884. Then with the new Martini-Henry carbine the regiment won the Lloyd Lindsay competition in 1886 and 1888 (coming second in 1887 when they took the Inter-Yeomanry Cup instead). The National Defence Act of 1888 extended their conditions of service to cover any part of the United Kingdom but the volunteers were spared any involvement in colonial expeditions until the Boer War at the end of the century. They left for South Africa as the 26th (Dorset) Company of the 7th Battalion, Imperial Yeomanry.

On the declaration of war in 1914 there were four sections of the Dorset Yeomanry:

> *'A-Squadron (Major Lord Wynford) at Dorchester. B-Squadron (Major John Goodden) at Sherborne. The Machine Gun Section (Captain V. C. M. Reeves) also at Sherborne. D-Squadron (Captain Sir Randolf Baker) at Gillingham.'*

Lieutenant-Colonel Edward Troyte-Bullock, of Zeals House, put them on a war footing. In September, Brigadier-General the 9th Earl of Shaftesbury called for volunteers to go overseas. There was an enthusiastic response and the men were attached to the 2nd South Midland Mounted Brigade under Brigadier-General the 5th Earl of Longford.

In May 1915, a second regiment of the Dorset Yeomanry was raised at Sherborne by Lieutenant-Colonel Thomas Colfox and attached to the 2/1st South-Western Mounted

Brigade. This had a coastal defence role in Sussex and Kent. In 1916 a 3/1st Queen's Own Dorset Yeomanry joined the first two regiments. Instead of being sent to France, as was expected, both of these units ended up in Ireland.

As for the original 1/1st Dorset Yeomanry, it was on Fakenham Common, Norfolk, on Christmas Day in 1914 and told to expect a German invasion. Then in April 1915 it was disembarking near Alexandria, in Egypt, and then joined the SS *Sarnia* at Lemnos to sail for Suvla Bay, in support of Winston Churchill's great Gallipoli gamble. In open formation, with the 2nd Mounted Division, they approached Chocolate Hill from La Baba on the night of 20 August 1915. At 16.20 hours on the 21st they were ordered to attack Scimitar Hill in support of the Berkshire Yeomanry. The Turks were firmly entrenched and fortified, with artillery, and overlooked sandy ground without any cover.

The DORSETS are coming !

The Dorset Yeomanry were to do it for real at Agagia, Libya.

As a result the fighting became suicidal. Seven out of the eight Dorset officers were injured or killed. Sixty per cent of their men became casualties. At 03.30 hours on 22 August the only surviving officer was told to withdraw. The remnants of the QODY fell-back to Chocolate Hill at 14.30 that afternoon. Their dead officers were Lieutenant Sir Thomas Lees and Captain Livingstone-Learmonth; missing were Lieutenant Gray and Lieutenant Kennaway; wounded were Lieutenant Bragge, Major Castleman and Major Reeves. The divisional commander, Major-General (Sir) William Peyton, witnessed the massacre:

> '... the forlorn hope charge into the Turkish trenches. I watched them go. I saw them fall in groups, and yet never a waver on the onward march. They secured themselves in spite of heavy losses in the front line Turkish trenches on Scimitar Hill. Never was a desperate attack more gallantly led; never was the call of a commander more bravely answered than by the men of the Dorset Yeomanry.'

It was the beginning of the end. Three weeks later the regiment was brought back to Alexandria where Major Goodden assumed command. On 11 October the Commander-in-Chief, Sir Ian Hamilton, declared that a general withdrawal was unthinkable, and as a result was recalled to London. He was replaced by Sir Charles Munro who brought plans for total evacuation before the onset of winter.

A composite squadron of Dorset, Berkshire and Buckinghamshire Yeomanry was ordered to El Daba, towards Libya, where they faced Senussi guerrillas – led by Sidi Ahmed – who were fighting alongside Turkish troops under the commanded of Kurdish General Ja'far Pasha-El Askari. They threatened to invade Europe. The QODY squadron defeated a small Senussi force at Ummrakham and joined a column of the Western Frontier Force under Brigadier-General Julian Tyndale-Biscoe.

Lieutenant-Colonel Hugh Maurice Wellesley Souter (1873-1941) commanded the regiment and Brigadier-General (Sir) Henry Lukin a mechanised column when air reconnaissance reported a Senussi force massing at Agagia, 14 miles south-east of Sidi Barrani. The Senussi tactics were to engage infantry positions from a strong point and then slip away into the desert. An estimated 2,500 Senussi were in a mile-long column with a thousand camels. On 26 February 1916, South African troops were attacked by the Senussi and Lukin ordered Souter's cavalry to swing inland and then come out of the desert, to thwart their retreat.

A total of 196 Dorset Yeomen were mustered, including the two regimental cooks, who brandished meat-cleavers instead of swords. Colonel Souter led the cavalry charge of the QODY. His horse was killed beneath him but with Lieutenant Blaksley and a trooper he went on to personally capture Ja'far Pasha and his staff. The vanquished general said:

'C'est magnifique mais ce n'est pas selon les regles.'

No one but the British cavalry could have done it, he added. The Dorset squadron lost 58 casualties (32 killed and 26 injured). The dead included Major Reeves, Lieutenant Bengough (attached to QODY from the Gloucester Yeomanry), and Second-Lieutenants Hope, Paulet and Middleton. Colonel Souter was awarded the Distinguished Service Order and Lieutenant Blaksley the Military Cross. The latter described the action:

'The Senussi were running in all directions, shrieking and yelling and throwing away their arms, the Yeomen after them. The whole thing was a marvellous instance of the awful terror inspired by galloping horses and steel. Some stood their ground and, by dodging the swords and shooting at two or three yards; range, first the horse and then our men, accounted for most of the casualties.'

General Peyton concurred:

'That charge, following a brilliant infantry attack, settled the small campaign – it was the Battle of Agagia in which the Dorset Yeomanry took so leading a part, which really sealed the fate of the combined Turks and Senussi who had contemplated an attack on Egypt and had for some months held a large British force in check. For Dorsetshire – February 26, 1916, should be an anniversary to remember.'

Brought back to strength by men from the 3/1st QODY, the regiment joined the 6th Mounted Brigade (re-named the Imperial Mounted Division) of the Egyptian Expeditionary Force. In the first Battle of Gaza they prevented Turkish reinforcements arriving from Hereir and covered the withdrawal across Wadi Ghuzze, under artillery fire. In June 1917 the new Commander-in-Chief, General Sir Edmund Allenby, ordered Brigadier-General Godwin to attack Turkish positions above the Gaza-Beersheba road at El Mughar. QODY and the Buckinghamshire Hussars formed up in Wadi Janus on 13 November.

They trotted a mile towards the Turks and then drew their swords. They went into a gallop for the last 1,000 yards but the horses found the slope too steep. Having dismounted, the Yeomanry squadrons moved forward on foot, taking several machine guns and many prisoners. Turkish morale collapsed as the Berkshire Yeomanry came up over the end of the ridge to round up stragglers. A total of 14 machine guns, two field guns and over 1,400 prisoners were taken.

In the next action, on 15 November, it was the turn of the QODY to gallop forward after their Bucks and Berks colleagues had fallen back from the ridge between Sidun and Abu Shusheh. Lieutenant-Colonel Sir Randolf Baker ordered C-Squadron to create a diversion while 'B' and 'A' Squadrons worked their way around to the flank of the position and charge from the rear. They successfully took 100 prisoners, two machine-guns, and a Krupp field-gun which Major Frederick Wingfield Digby took home – along with a DSO – as a trophy to Sherborne Castle. General Allenby described it as 'a brilliant attack by mounted troops'.

By 1918 the war was being wrapped up fast and QODY – as part of the 10th Cavalry Brigade – had its moments leading from the front, such as through the Sharon Gap in

The Krupp field-gun Major Frederick Wingfield Digby took back to Sherborne.

the orange groves north of Jaffa on 19 September 1918. Brigadier-General Wilfrith Gerald Key Green (1872-1937) took command after the brigade arrived at the Musmus Pass in the Samaritan Hills, during a night march, at 03.00 hours on 20 September. During the day Captain H. F. Yeatman was killed while facing 'well-trained troops from the direction of Aleppo' (Halab, Syria). That afternoon, however, QODY were first into Beisan, at the gallop through the village, where they took 100 prisoners, three 15-centimetre howitzers, and an arms cache.

Nablus was next, with 4,000 Turks being captured by the division, of whom 2,800 were processed by the QODY. They moved into Deraa and Lieutenant-Colonel G. K. M. Mason and Captain Lidderdale carried out a 'highly successful charge' to finish off a skirmish at El Remte, on 27 September, with 100 prisoners and four captured machine-guns.

On 28 September, a QODY patrol picked up two Arabs, one of whom spoke good English and asked to speak to the commanding officer. Lieutenant-Colonel Mason found his prisoner was Colonel T. E. Lawrence – the legendary Lawrence of Arabia. The end-game was in progress. The 4th and 5th Cavalry Divisions, the Desert Mounted Corps and Lawrence's Arab irregulars entered Damascus on 1 October. The QODY's war is documented in *Records of the Dorset Yeomanry 1914-19* by Major C. W. Thompson (1921) and *A Short Account of the Queen's Own Dorset Yeomanry 1794-1939* by Major R. H. Glyn.

There was a Dorset dimension to the Turkish Armistice as it was signed off the island of Mudros, in the battleship HMS *Agamemnon*, which had mobilised for war in Portland Harbour in 1914. Major-General Sir Charles Townshend and Admiral Wester Wemyss concluded the terms which came into effect at noon on 31 October 1918.

ten

1st Battalion, Dorsetshire Regiment

O N THE DAY that the world went to war, the 1st Battalion, Dorsetshire Regiment were already on a front line, being stationed in the Victoria Barracks, Belfast, as military support on the troubled island for the Royal Irish Constabulary. The order for mobilisation was received in the office of Captain Algernon Lee Ransome (1883-1969) at 05.39 hours on Tuesday 4 August 1914. At 08.00, detachments were sent to potentially vulnerable points as Woodburn and Stoneyford, and at 9.30 a party of officers left for the ferry to Strabane, en route home to Dorchester with the regimental colours – to be laid up in St Mary's Church – and arrived the following day. There, in the regimental depot beside Bridport Road, the advance party received a telegram from the War Office on 6 August, ordering them to leave for France ahead of their men. The battalion was to join the 15th Brigade in the British Expeditionary Force.

Back in Ireland, the battalion attended a special service in Belfast Cathedral on 13 August, and sailed the following day at 13.00 hours on the SS *Anthony*. She docked in Le Havre at 16.00 on Sunday 16 August. Horses had to be unloaded in a sling, one at a time, which delayed completion of disembarkation until 23.00 hours. Meanwhile the men marched uphill for a couple of hours, to No. 8 Camp, and were given a floral welcome by the French. That day Liege fell and the Belgians prepared to defend Antwerp. Captain R. G. B. M. Hyslop, the billeting officer, managed to purloin a 70-horsepower Daimler as he organised the move towards the front:

> *'There was time to get everything cut and dried before the units began to arrive, and from going to the villages so often one got on very friendly terms with the mayors, who always pressed one to have lunch with them.'*

He found himself over-loaded with 'champagne, beer and wine, chocolates and all sorts of things, which they pressed on us'. Once the men had all been sent off on trains, there seemed nothing left to do, 'so we went and had dinner'. All that changed after arrival at Dour, at dusk on 22 August, to scenes of 'great confusion'. He caught up with the battalion's A-Company in a factory at Boussu. D-Company was already almost in sight of the enemy, having marched to Ors on the Sambre Canal on 18 August, where they placed guards on the north side of this 'very pretty village' to prepare for the arrival of German cavalry.

The Dorsets were in the advance guard of 15th Infantry Brigade when it moved forward at dawn – at 04.00 – on the hot morning of 21 August. They took up positions at Gommegneis. The next move was to Dou, in a 15-mile march, where on the 22nd British intelligence warned of 'German masses approaching' and General Sir John French decided to use his 36,000 men to hold the strategic line along the Mons Canal. French had only a relatively small force – with which he had hoped to outflank the Germans – but found himself facing an unstoppable onslaught.

On Sunday 23 August, early morning cavalry patrols brushed with the enemy, and the German guns opened up shortly before 09.00. The Battle of Mons had begun. Sustained British rifle-fire held back the Germans, but 330 British soldiers died during the day, and more than 1,250 were injured.

On the 24th the Germans crossed the canal at Mariette and forced the Dorsets back via Paturages to Blaugies. Captain Hyslop and two other officers were wounded and taken prisoner. Twelve Dorsets were killed, 49 injured, and 69 reported missing. Captain Ransome reviewed the day:

> *'Confused fighting, complicated by uncertainly as regards the flanks, lack of training in street fighting, and embarrassment over the crowds of civilians thronging the streets. The enemy was well supported with artillery and machine-guns, added to which his superior numbers enabled him to push through the many gaps in our line under cover of the numerous avenues of approach which this industrial area afforded.'*

On the 25th the Dorsets started marching at 02.00 hours, along the straight and seemingly endless Roman road to Le Cateau, where they eventually rested in a corn-field. Ransome described the experience:

> *'It was crowned with inhabitants hurrying south-westwards, carrying bundles and wheeling their belongings in carts and barrows. The effect was depressing and brought home only too clearly what retreat entailed.'*

Ransome established his battalion headquarters in a cottage at la Sotaire. Next day Inchy was in flame at midday after 'a terrific cannonade' and the Suffolks saw most of the fighting. Lieutenant C. H. Woodhouse held the Dorset section of the line with a machine-gun. Then Lieutenant-Colonel (Sir) Loius Jean Bols (1867-1930) felt they were too exposed. The battalion fell back to Ponchaux for a brief rest, but at 03.00 on the 27th they were on the road again, to Estrees. Their 40-mile withdrawal continued to St Quentin, and then resumed, to Eaucourt on the south side of the River Somme.

1ST BATTALION, DORSETSHIRE REGIMENT

'Two drummers played their flutes,' the regimental history records. Before dawn on the 28th they were marching once more. Sir John French, the Commander-in-Chief, was at the roadside to promise of 'three days' rest'. Next stop was Pontoise on the south bank of the River Oise. Then in the afternoon they were shifted to Carlepont and at 02.20 on the 30th the retreat resumed. The battalion crossed the River Aisne at Attichy and stopped on the ridge beyond, at Croutoy, at 08.00.

Hardly anything had been heard of the Germans for days but marching resumed at 07.30 on the 31st which turned into 'another tropical day'. The trek around Compiegne Forest ended in bivouacs at Crepy-en-Valois at 18.00. On 1 September the day was spent in some confusion, marching down the valley to Duvy, and then sideways to Ormoy Villers, after rumours that German cavalry were in the vicinity.

The wider strategic position was that the 15th Brigade had evaded an 'enveloping attack' by the German First and Second Armies, and were now defending the outskirts of Paris. Belgian refugees poured into the capital and similar numbers of its residents fled south and west. Meanwhile the French counter-attacked at Guise and landings of the Royal Marine Brigade at Ostend – rumoured to be Russians 'with snow on their boots' – was thought by the enemy to be much more than a diversion. *The Times* had done wonders with that story of 'carriages packed with fierce-looking bearded fellows in fur hats' but its correspondent in Amiens, Arthur Moore, shocked the nation with news of the 'terrible defeat' that had left 'broken bits of many regiments' who were 'battered by marching'.

In fact it was the Germans who were over-extended, and chasing an elusive enemy to beyond the River Marne, where on 4 September the combined Anglo-French forces were ready to respond. The Dorsets turned around, setting off northwards, at 05.00 on 6 September. In all, in the retreat from Mons, the Dorsets had marched 220 miles in 16 days.

Their first positive action, on the afternoon of the 9th, was to secure an artillery battery on Hill 189, in the woods at Pisseloup, above the River Marne. Forty-seven dead Germans were found on the ridge. Battalion losses were three officers and seven other ranks dead, 31 wounded, and four missing.

On 23 September the men dug front line trenches to defend the village of Missy on the south bank of the Aisne. Deadlock had begun. On 1 October the Dorsets returned to Jury and next day they entered Launoy at midnight. Night marches were the norm, Ransome recorded:

> 'The utmost secrecy was maintained. No hint of the actual destination was given. The wildest rumours were in circulation; Antwerp, and even England, were suggested as the ultimate goal.'

On the following days they went through Corcy, Fresnoy la Riviere and Verberie, reaching Compiegne Station on the 7th. The train left for Abbeville, and from there they marched to Genne Ivergny, arriving there on the evening of the 8th. On 10 October they were at Haravesnes the day that Antwerp fell. The Dorsets were told to hold the canal near Bethune as the Germans advanced on Auchy. Major R. T. Roper was killed on the 12th while on a recce from Pont Fixe. Several others were also hit by snipers and Captain's Ransome's machine-gun section faced a German howitzer. Skirmishing turned into a battle on the 13th.

The 1st Battalion lost four officers killed, seven wounded, and four missing. Of the other ranks, 14 were killed, 122 wounded, and 84 missing. Burial parties over the next few days accounted for 130 dead. Lieutenant-Colonel Bols and Lieutenant Pitt held their trench but Captain F. H. B. Rathborne crawled back severely wounded. Major C. Saunders and Captain Beveridge assumed command of the battalion and continued to hold the canal at Pont Fixe until relieved by the Devons on the 15th. They moved barely a mile, to Rue d'Ouvert, and started digging trenches.

Lieutenant Woodhouse was captured on the 22nd while going to the aid of a nearby detachment of the Cheshires. It was a confusing situation after the Germans attacked in the mist with 'whiz-bangs and oil-cans'. Captain Beveridge was seen to be wounded and then reported missing. Seven men were killed, 24 others wounded, and a total of 102 missing.

From here the battalion moved to Richbourg St Vaast and at the end of the month were in Strazeele. The mobile war was over, as far as the Western Front was concerned, and the battalion settled into the stalemate of the trenches. During the winter of 1914-15, they held 'the ditch' at Wulverghem, Ypres, with companies taking their turn with rest periods at Neuve Eglise, Dranoutre and Bailleul. In the summer of 1915 they moved south to what was then the quiet sector on the River Somme.

During the Battle of Gravenstafel Ridge, on 22-23 April 1915, the Dorsets were holding the front line from the Buff to the Ypres-Comines railway. They took casualties in the bombardment that proceeded the second Battle of Ypres. Major Cowie had the battalion construct a new trench to the south of Kruisstraat – the Hooge Switch – as a contingency measure.

On 29 April the battalion was ordered to relieve the 2nd Camerons on the slope of Hill 60, beside the railway in the Zwarteleen salient. This was not going to be a picnic, as Captain Rawsome realised, though much worse followed:

> *'The approach to the front line was an unpleasant experience. The Germans were employing a thorough programme of harassing fire. The canal bridges, all roads and tracks, and finally the railway cutting leading to Hill 60, were under incessant shell-fire. The support position consisted of shelters dug into the hillside and covered with corrugated iron and sandbags.'*

The horror came with clouds of yellow and white poison gas that drifted across from 19.15 hours. C-Company, on top of the hill, were particularly affected. The deadly thing was to seek relief in the trenches (as the gas was heavier than air). It asphyxiated those who crouched down whereas Second-Lieutenant Kestell-Cornish had the presence of mind to persuade four of his men to keep their heads high and disperse the cloud by firing into it. He was awarded the Military Cross. Many were dying in agony but there was no German attack on the ground. Major Cowie inspected the Dorset lines and found a total of 53 dead, 206 poisoned, and 32 missing. One hundred of the injured were to succumb and the missing had also gone off to die.

Some of the gas drifted back across the German lines, causing them to retreat rather than advance, though after the Dorsets had been relieved the enemy took what was described as 'a mere rubbish heap of shell and mine-torn earth, timber and dead bodies'. On 6 May, when it withdrew to bivouacs at Kruisstraat, the fighting strength of the battalion had been reduced from 800 to 173 all ranks. Such was the replenishment rate, however, that when it returned to the Hill 60 sector on 20 May, Captain Ransome was put in command of a battalion 1,100-strong.

The situation stabilised with growing sophistication and a system of fortifications in depth on each side of no man's land. There were now triple lines, with communications trenches linking them, and strong-points – or redoubts – at regular intervals. The Commander-in-Chief of the British Expeditionary Force, General Sir Douglas Haig, would lead a total of 1,343,457 men on the eve of the Battle of the Somme.

Bapaume remained in German hands for most of the war.

In 1916 the 1st Battalion, Dorsetshire Regiment was transferred from the 5th Division to the 32nd Division (to join the 95th Infantry Brigade which was renamed the 14th Infantry Brigade on 7 January). It was to hold Authuille on the River Ancre. They moved on to Frechencourt and Millencourt, and marched through shell-torn Albert with its statuette of the Virgin and Child poised at 'a miraculous angle' on the church tower. Lieutenant C. O. G. Douie described the positions towards Authuille and Aveluy Wood in February:

> *'East of the cemetery was the heaped white chalk of several mine craters. Above them lay the shattered tree trunks and litter of brick which had once been the village of la Boisselle. We progressed slowly down the remains of a trench and came to the craters and the sap* [covered or ziz-zag trench] *which ran between them. Here there was no trench, only sandbags, one layer thick, and about two feet above the top of the all-prevailing mud …*

> *'We crawled away and came in time to a trench behind the cemetery, known as Gowrie Street. Liquid lime washed over and above our knees; tree trunks, riven into strange shapes, lay over and alongside the trench. The wintry day imposed a greyness over all. The shattered crosses of the cemetery lay at every angle about the torn graves. The trenches were alive with men, but no sign of life appeared over the surface of the ground. Even the grass was withered by the fumes of high-explosives.'*

An incursion across no man's land, known as the Y-Sap Raid – off the Bapaume road at la Boisselle – took place after a mine had been exploded on the afternoon of 26 March 1916. Experienced hands sensed that the Germans knew the Dorsets were coming, and the men duly advanced into an empty trench and an ambush, which left many wounded.

Having been moved along the line, and given a month's rest and training, the battalion under Major J. V. Shute returned to the Thiepval sector at the end of April. D-Company came under a half-hour bombardment from trench mortars at 23.30 on 7 May. A German raid left 13 men killed, 31 wounded, and 24 missing. There would be further casualties. Lieutenant Douie described how 'the great mass of Thiepval Wood' was 'never silent' as 'shell and rifle-fire echoed endlessly through the trees'.

Two long-term officers were lost on 17 May. Captain W. B. Algeo and Lieutenant H. G. M. Mansel-Pleydell – 'an incomparable intelligence officer' – went off on a daylight recce from Hammehead Sap. They never returned. Sergeant W. Goodwillie and Sergeant Rogers went in search of them. Goodwillie was also killed and Rogers had to fight his way back.

On 1 July 1916, the fateful day for the Somme offensive, the 14th Brigade was tasked to support the 32nd Division in the Battle of Albert. The advance was to be from Crowbent Street and Union Street, towards Mouquet Farm and the Goat Redoubt. The Dorsets moved to Blackhorse Bridge where numerous reconnaissances had been made. Douie found morale was high:

> *'The proceedings were marked by no high seriousness, and occasionally degenerated into hilarity … This reached its climax when a young officer received instructions that his duty was to convey a Bangalore torpedo up to and beyond Mouquet Farm, to place it under the wire of the German third line and, having exploded it, to consolidate beyond this somewhat advanced position.'*

Breakfast on the 1st was at 06.30 and by 07.10 platoons were heading through Authuille Wood, along the Dumbarton Track. Zero hour was 07.30 when the regimental history records that 'the air throbbed' with 'an incredible volume of sound' as trench mortars rained 'a hurricane discharge'. There was so much wire that the men had to make an exposed dash 'through a hail of bullets' before 'they reached our own front line, let alone the enemy's'. Drum-Major Kerr encouraged them forward, to the strains of the flute, playing the regimental march-past. Oblivious of the risk, he 'continued to play well-known tunes, until his left arm was shattered by a bullet'.

Only 25 men reached the German front line. They found remnants of the 11th Border Regiment, without any officers, and some Lancashire Fusiliers, who were ordered to withdraw. Then Lieutenant C. G. Butcher, with three Second-Lieutenants and 85 other ranks, found he was holding the British front line – without anyone on either side – and hunkered down under heavy fire. At 17.00, Major H. D. Thwaytes reached the trench and took command, until the Dorsets were relieved during the night by the 15th Highland Light Infantry.

Sixty Dorsets had been killed. It was the day that the British Army suffered its worst-ever losses with 19,240 dead, 2,152 missing presumed dead, 585 taken prisoner, and 35,493 wounded.

1ST BATTALION, DORSETSHIRE REGIMENT

The following night the Dorsets held the old British front line between Tindrum Street and Chequerbent Street and carried ammunition and bombs forward to the Highlanders who were fighting in the adjoining Leipzig salient. They then fell back to Senlis, Forceville and Bouzincourt, on 7 July, as the official despatch recorded the failure of the offensive:

> '... the enemy's continued resistance at Thiepval and Beaumont Hamel made it impossible to send forward reinforcements and ammunition, and, in spite of their gallant efforts, our troops were forced to withdraw during the night to their own lines.'

The battalion held a low-lying part of the line, at Bethune, through into the wet autumn of 1916 when positions had to be evacuated due to waist-deep mud and water. Trench-foot became a common complaint with the only half-cure being liberal smearing of whale-oil. Such conditions dampened aggressive tendencies. Then the battalion moved to Mailly Maillet.

It split in order to support an attack at Beaumont Hamel on 17 November. A-Company supported the 15th Highland Light Infantry and B and D-Companies (under Captain Kestell-Cornish) backed the 2nd Manchesters. Their attacks failed and the Dorsets were left in the old front line. By the 19th its muddy trenches were collapsing and the battalion suffered a continuing attrition rate – with 13 killed, 72 wounded, and 18 missing.

The 1st Dorsets took part in the offensive at Arras in March 1916.

The battalion was withdrawn to Mailly Maillet and spent December resting in Berteau-court. General Haig intended to attack the salient between the River Ancre and Arras after 1 February 1917. In the event, anticipating this, the German High Command pulled its forces back in Operation Alberich which began on 16 March 1916. Plans evolved for the British to follow them into Flanders, beginning the offensive at Messines and continuing to Ypres, as conscription at home brought ever-increasing numbers of troops into France. National Registration was instituted in 1915, for all males aged 15 and upwards, with telegrams to be expected as they reached their 18th birthdays.

In August 1916, the British Army in France and Flanders numbered 2,044,627 – its highest figure in history – with 6,304 field guns, 2,936 trench-mortars and an ammunition supply rate of a million rounds a week.

External events included a revolution in Russia and the entry of the United States into the war on 6 April 1917. For the Dorsets, Captain G. N. Wood wrote, the 'bottom-less mud' of the Ancre valley made an offensive impossible, but on average there were 'some 20 or 30 casualties from shell-fire during each four days' spell in the front line'. They had been holding Ten Tree Alley between Beaumont Hamel and Serre.

Following the German retreat the battalion set off across devastated countryside and B-Company hastily built a 'Dorset Bridge' across the canal at Rouy le Grand. On 21 March they marched into Matigny. Most of their time was spent filling 'potholes' – in the form of huge craters that the enemy had left at every cross-roads. The village of Holnon was reached on 3 April 1917. The next line, on 13 April, was between the Bois des Roses and St Quentin which was coming under French attack. In a 'rushed' action, Captain Hands of C-Company was ordered at 06.30 hours by Major Butcher to take Cepy Farm, on a key road into the town:

> *'You see that farm? Well, I want you to capture it now, at once.'*

D. Stayner described the operation as 'magnificent to watch' with the line going 'forward in one long swing, at a slow job trot'. The Germans kept firing until the men

Ypres, after two years of war, as the 1st Dorsets saw it.

were within 50 yards, and then fled, leaving the battalion in possession by 09.00. At counter-attack took place the following day, at 15.00, after a day-long bombardment. This was fought off with the loss of 15 men dead and 25 wounded. The battalion was then relieved and moved back to Savy, Ugny and Lanchy.

On 17 June, the Dorsets were unexpectedly ordered north, to take over from the French in sand-dunes on the coast between Nieuport and Oost-Dunkerque. Captain W. A. Smellie initially welcomed the move:

> *'It was very pleasant being near the sea and the sector at that time was very quiet. The men enjoyed bathing, although it was restricted afterwards to certain areas owing to German artillery shelling bathing parties.'*

Battalion headquarters was in a concrete pill-box, known as the Rubber Hut, which withstood hits from 5.9-inch shells. Elsewhere, however, there was very little cover and much flooding, with Nieuport being subject to nightly attacks from gas-shells. Trench-mortars had demolished much of the breastworks which had been left in a poor state of repair.

On 10 July, the Germans attacked Nieuport and advanced to the River Yser, though they were then forced back and only succeeded in holding the Nose Lane support trench in the polders to the north of the town. Having relieved a Highland battalion, the Dorsets had four men killed and 26 wounded.

Major H. C. Lloyd took command of the battalion and intensified its training during periods behind the line at la Panne. Captain Smellie recalled a number of excellent dinners in the Tirlink Hotel at Dunkerque. The 32nd Division were held in reserve until the last attack at Passchendaele in the nightmare third Battle of Ypres.

Then they were thrown into the attack, into the featureless mud from Wurst Farm to the east of St Julien, at 01.55 on 2 December 1917. By the end of the day they had been kicked back to where they started. No further offensive actions were anticipated. On the 3rd, the Dorsets relieved the 16th Northumberland Fusiliers, on the front line. Battalion headquarters were at Virile Farm. Major Thwaytes described almost unendurable cold, in a barren landscape 'sodden and ploughed up by shellfire', which was crossed only by duck-board tracks. Heavy snow on 25 December conveniently cancelled orders to attack a pillbox. On 27 December the division was pulled back to Nielles-les-Ardresthe, for three weeks, to rest and celebrate a belated Christmas.

From there the men returned to Ypres, to Houthulst Forest, from where C and D-Companies were tasked with the Royal Scots to raid German positions near Surcouff Farm on 27 January 1918. Brigade commander Brigadier-General Frederick Lumsden VC, DSO, joined the enterprise. Five pill-boxes were overrun with the loss of four Dorset dead, two missing and 29 wounded.

The Dorsets were in the front line at Grutersaele, to the south of Arras, when the Germans launched their big offensive on 21 March with a five-hour artillery barrage. The battalion diary hardly gives it a mention:

> *'No unusual event. Two other ranks killed, 14 wounded,'*

The battalion was relieved on 27th and in turn took over from the 11th East Lancashires near Ayette on the 31st. It was at the extreme right flank of General Erich Ludendorff's advance. Ayette village was recaptured by Highlanders, supported by C-Company of the Dorsets, and the biggest danger came from stray shells. One killed Major T. W. Bullock, outside battalion headquarters at Douchy, on 12 April. On the 14th the battalion suffered 100 casualties from an overnight gas-attack with delayed-action shells.

What has been described as 'one of the finest raids of the war' began at 03.00 on 21 May. B and D-Companies, led by Captain Bower – who carried on despite being wounded – attacked deep dugouts along a bank at Hamelincourt. More than 50 Germans were killed. The battalion had 84 killed and wounded.

General Lumsden, who watched the raid, was killed by a sniper while visiting the front line on 3 June 1918. He was buried at Berles au Bois.

The 1st Dorsets went to rest billets at Bavingcourt on 6 July. They headed on foot to Mendicourt on the 18th and went by train to Waayenburg on the 19th. From there they marched to Oost Cappelle. They moved from Forrinoy to Domart on 8 August, to Beaucourt on the 9th, and forward to the front line facing Damery on the 10th.

That night, while bivouacked at le Quesnoy, they were ordered to 'capture and hold Damery village and Damery Wood'. The battalion was allocated a 2,000-yard front and told to attack at 09.20 on 11 August. All four companies were deployed (Left – B-Company; centre – A-Company; right – C-Company; extreme right – D-Company). Lieutenant-Colonel Thwaytes, as he became, records that C-Company was thrown into disarray by two 5.9-inch shells just minutes before zero hour though they soon regained their composure:

'I was an eye-witness to the move forward and as these companies stepped over the parapet they were met with a deadly and concentrated machine-gun fire from Parvillers. It seemed like a miracle that the whole battalion was not decimated on the starting line. An anti-tank gun, concealed in a corn-field, put six of the eight tanks sent up to assist the brigade out of action almost immediately. Within five minutes of zero the companies were well forward and lost to view in the standing crops.'

The Germans ran from Damery Wood but held out in the village to its left. C-Company veered to its left, and D-Company swung round in their place, capturing a German machine-gun and four prisoners. The two tanks also reached the village and Captain Hamilton pulled his men back to the old German front line to secure it for the night. They held off a counter-attack at dusk and a second attack during the night.

C and B-Companies met in Payen Copse and came under heavy enemy machine-gun fire from the next village to the left, at Parvillers. The fight had not be co-ordinated by the British General Headquarters with their counterparts, notably General Mathieu, in the adjoining French command. Captain Fell, the unfortunately liaison officer trying to sort out the mess, told his General Staff Officer:

'I don't think he proposes to budge, Sir. He thinks he's been let down!'

Captain Fell and his French counterpart, named Aublin, ventured by car along the road to report the situation on the ground. They came across a British brigadier with field glasses and a Dorset officer nursing a wounded arm. Neither knew anything of what was happening in Damery. The officers ventured close enough to the smoke surrounding Damery to see some khaki figures. Back with General Mathieu, after a lump of shell-casing had hit his heel, Captain Fell returned to General Mathieu's head-quarters and succeeded in co-ordinating a planned British attack (16.30) with a French attack (17.30) so that there could be a combined attack (at 18.00 hours).

The attack failed and the 3rd Canadian Division took over the line. The Dorsets marched back to Beaucourt. The battalion casualty list was 31 killed, 42 missing, 247 wounded and 1 gassed. There was a rest period at Domart.

The division came under Australian command and 'side-slipped to the north' on 18 August. The Germans were falling back and the battalion moved through Berny Wood, across Misery Ridge, and on the to the cross-roads at devastated and flattened Villers Carbonnel, to the line facing Happlincourt. There, on the night of 31 August, German aeroplanes dropped two bombs, killing the Quartermaster, Captain W. Alderman, who had been with the battalion since November 1914. Twenty horses were also killed and two transport men wounded. .

In September the battalion advanced – mostly by bus – to Daours, Athies, Larris Wood and Leverguier Ridge. In la Fleche Wood, near Levergies, they captured 380 prisoners, three 12-inch howitzers, five 4.2-inch field guns and five machine-guns. From 3-5 October, led by Major C. H. Morris, they fought the Battle of the Beaurevoir Line, from Levergies, in support of the Royal Scots. A-Company, under Captain C. J. Lonsdale, 'promptly charged the enemy, bayoneting 25 and driving a large number in front of them' but was forced to a standstill as 'further waves of Germans came round both flanks'.

Battalion casualties as a whole were heavy, with four officers killed, one missing, one taken prisoner, and four wounded. A total of 307 other ranks were killed, wounded or missing. On the other hand they had captured Sequehart where enemy dead 'were thick at the outer end of the village' and taken over 200 prisoners, plus 'a great number of machine-guns'. On 5 October the battalion was relieved by the Sherwood Foresters and marched backed to Lehaucourt. At the end of the month they advanced to St Souplet and swapped positions with the Foresters on the front line along the Sambre Canal.

Here the 32nd Division was tasked to force the canal, between Landrecies and Catillon, on 4 November. The Dorsets were ordered to cross it from Ors, at 05.45:

> '... after a hurricane of bombardment by the Stokes mortars, and a few smoke shells from the artillery, which intensified the natural morning mist.'

Second-Lieutenant H. N. Usher and a platoon of C-Company rushed forward with Sappers to span the gaps in a blown-up old bridge. To the south, Captain Lipscomb with two platoons of C-Company covered Royal Engineers, as they constructed a floating bridge. An attempted northern crossing, led by Second-Lieutenant F. C. Cassalman, failed when a collapsible boat capsized. Lieutenant L. H. Tirrell, manning the Dorset headquarters, organised the successful crossing of C and D-Companies together with the 2nd Manchesters.

The Dorsets took 223 prisoners, three 4.2-inch howitzers, and 30 machine-guns. Battalion losses were six killed and 50 men wounded. *The History of the Dorsetshire Regiment, 1914-19*, sums it up in a sentence:

> 'So far as the battalion was concerned the war was over.'

Not only that, the war was literally ending where it had started. Those few who had been with the 1st Battalion for the duration expressed feelings deja vu, on commencing that last engagement, in the Battle of Sambre. It was from Ors that they first faced the advancing Germans on 18 August 1914.

eleven

2nd Battalion, Dorsetshire Regiment

WITH THE MOTTO of the regiment being 'Primus in Indis' – 'First in India' – it was appropriate that on the declaration of war the 2nd Battalion, Dorsetshire Regiment, was quartered at Poona as part of an Indian division. It was under Lieutenant-Colonel H. L. Rosher with Major B. St John Clarkson second in command and Lieutenant F. G. Powell as adjutant. The first wartime order, on 14 August 1914, was to prepare to leave for East Africa – taking only machine-gun and water-carrying mules – with everything else going into store.

Events overtook the order, and by the time they eventually moved from Poona to Bombay, on October 12, it was to sail for the Persian Gulf where the Anglo-Persian oil-fields were threatened by the Ottoman Empire's ever closer links with the axis Central Powers. The battalion was to secure the vital British oil-field at Abadan.

A total of 22 officers, 5 warrant officers and 869 other ranks sailed on the British-India liner *Varela* on 18 October in a convoy of 54 ships shepherded by the old battle-ship HMS *Ocean*. Overcrowded, and sharing their space with support troops, they anchored off Bahrein in the heat for more than a week while awaiting further orders. Herbert Asquith's Government feared a precipitate decision would push Turkey into the war. In the event it was the bombardments of Russian Black Sea ports, by the Germans, and of the Dardanelles forts and Turkish Red Sea port of Akaba, by the British, that propelled Constantinople to declare war on 2 November.

The Dorsets, along with 3,600 other British and Indian troops, took Fao in the Turkish province of Mesopotamia on 7 November. Boats carrying C and D-Companies, under Major F. W. Radcliffe, were the first to land and push forward through palm groves as the local Turks fled from their mud fort. Towards Abadan there several skirmishes and Private Cumming, 'a big red-haired man' was congratulated by Major Radcliffe on being the first to bayonet a Turk. He replied:

2ND BATTALION, DORSETSHIRE REGIMENT

'Oh yes, Sir, but he was only a very little one.'

Six men had died in the early skirmishing and the battalion lost Major A. A. Mercer and Captain F. Middleton, plus 21 other ranks killed, and 149 wounded in evicting 5,000 Turks from Basra. They entered its 'labyrinth of incredibly dirty and evil-smelling streets' on November 21. The battalion proceeded to Al Qurnah, at the strategic confluence of the Euphrates and the Tigris, a fortnight later. More than a thousand Turks were taken prisoner and became known as the 'Catch 'em alive o's' from the daily routine reminder that there was to be no unnecessary killing.

The battalion went native with its transportation, venturing into flooded marshlands in shallow-draught 'bellums' and establishing a camel corps for desert patrols, under Lieutenant G. D. Yeatman and Lieutenant D. A. Simmons. Cavalry waded through rising water to reach Shaiba, and then pushed ahead to Shwaibda, on reports that Turkish reinforcements were advancing from the west in February 1915. Though facing an uncomfortable mix of floods, sandstorms, flies and mirages they succeeded in driving off a massed attack from Arab irregulars in what was described as:

'A regular Buffalo Bill show.'

Co-ordinated Turkish opposition did not materialise until 12 April. The following two days the Dorsets counter-attacked from Shaiba. Gradually both sides lost momentum in the heat and the Turks held the advantage with the lie of the land. At 14.30 on the 14th, as he paced up and down trying to work out where to send rein-forcements, Colonel Rosher was hit and killed by a bullet. Lieutenant-Colonel Clarkson took command and was wounded leading an advance on the 16 April which coincided with carts coming over the horizon, in order to take the wounded, being mistaken for the 16th Brigade charging to the battalion's rescue. The Turks retreated but the weary Dorsets, almost out of ammunition, were unable to follow them.

Fours officers were killed and 11 wounded. The battalion had effectively lost a quarter of its strength. Seven Distinguished Conduct Medals were awarded. General Sir John Nixon had arrived to take charge of the Mesopotamian Expeditionary Force and the 2nd Dorsets waded through floods to return to Basra. These were set to worsen. The battalion found itself washed out of its camp at Makina Masus on 10 May and took refuge in a liquorice factory. By the end of the month, nearly 200 men were hospi-talised from dysentery, fever and heat-stroke and the fighting strength of the battalion was down to 400 men. Eight additional detachments, each of an officer and 29 men, were found as reinforcements.

Major-General (Sir) Charles Vere Ferrers Townshend (1861-1924) arrived as the new General Officer Commanding. It was 'in boiling heat' that the battalion sailed on the river steamer – the *Medijieh* – for Al Qurnah on 28 May to take part in 'Townshend's Regatta'. They had been training in their bellums for an amphibious attack in marshes to the north. In the event, to the battalion's relief, the Turks withdrew, and they landed on Bahran Island – a 'poisonous place' – to find their enemy was the extreme heat. Major W. A. C. Fraser died of heat-stroke at Basra on 14 June; that month 114 men were invalided out of the battalion.

Townshend had further aspirations, and was planning an advance to Amara, but that was carried out by the 17th Brigade. Just one member of the battalion took part, on board the armed paddle-steamer *Comet*. From here, General Nixon was keen to moved forward to Es Sinn and the key position it protected, at Kut al Amara beside the junction of the Tigris and the Shatt al Hai waterway. The 17th Brigade and two battalions of the 16th Brigade were to be led by General Hoghton. The rest of 16th Brigade (including the 2nd Dorsets) formed a 'General Reserve'.

The main column took a wrong direction, taking them away from the action for a day, and leaving the Dorsets to stumble upon the 'northern redoubt' of the Turkish defences. The battalion comprised A-Company (Captain G. M. Herbert), B-Company (Captain W. Clemson), C-Company (Major H. K. Utterson) and D-Company (Captain Mortimore). Mortimore and his platoon were first into the redoubt. Seventeen men were killed or missing and 143 wounded. Soon the battalion had gathered 130 prisoners and won praise from General Townshend:

> *'The Dorsets, as usual, covered themselves with glory.'*

The 16th Brigade moved down to the River Tigris and the 17th Brigade entered Kut, on 28 September 1915, as the Turks withdrew. River levels were low, hazarding the flow of supplies, so thoughts of pushing on to Baghdad were abandoned. On 22 November, half the battalion (under Major Utterson) advanced under artillery and sniper fire to within sight of the great Arch of Ctesiphon. This too pleased General Townshend who is quoted from *My Campagn in Mesopotamia*:

> *'In all my experience of war, I have never seen or heard of anything so fine as the deliberate and tranquil advance of the thin chain of Dorsets in extended order, moving south from the vantage point – the Turks in bunches evacuating trenches in front of them.'*

The Turks, however, moved their reserves forward – Baghdad being only 25 miles away – whereas General Townshend had none, and the Dorsets kept up such continuous fire that grease bubbled from the woodwork of their Lee-Enfield rifles and the sights became too hot to touch. Finally, all the mules were killed and there was no more ammunition, and the captured Turkish guns had to be abandoned, as there was no way of hauling them back. The Dorsets had lost nine officers and over 200 other ranks. Captain Mortimore was among the dead. All units were down to half strength or less. But the Turks had suffered more and were in no mood to counter-attack until they realised, a day later, that the British unable to resume the offensive.

General Townshend concentrated his remaining troops in former Turkish strong-points around Ctesiphon. On 25 November the enemy regained their old trenches at Diyala and carried out repeated attacks on the British-held 'water redoubt'. River transport was needed for the wounded and the retreat to Aziziya was being watched by the Arabs. General Townshend realised he had to attack, to deter Turkish harassment, and British guns found 'a splendid artillery target' at daylight on 1 December. This put the enemy into confusion and the British retreat resumed. A forced-march of 18 miles put some distance between them and the pursuers.

2ND BATTALION, DORSETSHIRE REGIMENT

Kut Day in Dorchester, remembering the troops in Mesopotamia, 26 July 1916.

Two gun-boats and a barge, loaded with 300 wounded, ran aground in the Tigris and had to be abandoned. The steamer *T2* was also grounded for several hours – under fire from Arabs on the riverbank – until her Indian crew managed to pull her free. On 3 December 1915, the 6th Division had fallen back to Kut, having covered 80 miles in a week. The following day they set about digging fortifications. From the 2nd Dorsets, under rapidly promoted Lieutenant-Colonel G. M. Herbert, there were 12 officers, 315 other ranks, and 134 men in hospital.

A senior German officer, 72-year-old Field-Marshal Baron Kolmar von der Goltz, was on his way to take command of 30,000 Turkish reinforcements. That took Turkish forces to 80,000, bearing down on 25,000 British and Indian troops in Kut, occupying an ox-bow peninsula on the Tigris. The siege began on 5 December 1915. As with the Suvla and Anzac beaches in Gallipoli, from where the British Cabinet ordered an evacuation on 7 December, the Mesopotamian thrust towards Baghdad was becoming a defeat and humiliation. Exciting adventures had turned into depressing reverses.

The defenders held out for 147 days. Turkish attempts at storming the defences were fought off, though often at some cost, such as on 13 December when the Dorsets lost Lieutenant Joy, who was killed, and Lieutenant Corrall, who died from his wounds. Starvation became the more immediate threat.

The relief force never reached them but not through want of trying. It lost 4,000 dead and injured when it was intercepted at Sheikh Sa'ad. A thousand wounded were still lying there in the mud, a week later, when they reached by an Indian Field Ambulance unit. Two hundred Anglo-Indian troops were killed and 1,000 wounded in the Battle of Wadi, on 13 January 1916. Then, on the 21st, there were 2,600 casualties at the Battle of Hanna. British officers in that action included a future Prime Minister, Captain Clement Attlee – wounded in the buttocks – and Robert Palmer, a grandson of former Prime Minister Lord Salisbury and cousin of Sir Edward Grey, the Foreign Secretary. Palmer, who was killed, had a prophetic poem published in *The Times* ('How Long, O Lord?') in the autumn.

Too much water, along a flooded Tigris, impeded relief efforts though one attempt nearly broke through. Within sight of Kut's minarets, at Dujaila on 7 March 1916, 3,500 men were killed or wounded on 7 March 1916. Lieutenant-General Sir Fenton Aylmer was retired as a result. Then came an heroic gesture, when the paddle-steamer *Julnar*, with 270 tons of supplies, ran the gauntlet of the Tigris but was spiked by steel and wire defences. Lieutenant-Commander Cowley (executed by the Turks) and Lieutenant H. O. B. Firman (died in captivity) were awarded the Victoria Cross.

Hunger brought about the inevitable, after the last animal had been eaten, and the men received a final air-dropped treat of a piece of chocolate and four ounces of bread. Kut's suffering Dorsetmen on the ground had their own Netherbury hero in the air. Captain Campbell Sanctuary volunteered to transfer from the Royal Field Artillery to the Royal Flying Corps and became an air-gunner. His role over starving Kut, flying in low, was to drop as much food as the light aircraft could carry. He then qualified as a pilot in what by the Armistice was the Royal Air Force.

General Townshend surrendered Kut on 29 April 1916. More than 9,000 men became prisoners and were joined by 2,500 captives from the relief columns. They were marched out of the town on 6 May, to cover 15 miles without water or shade, and the second day many were forced to continue without shoes. Those who flagged were beaten by Arab mercenaries. From the opposite bank of the river, Captain E. O. Moulsey described prisoners 'dying with a green ooze issuing from their lips, their mouths fixed open, in and out of which flies walked'. The horrors and endurance of the 2,000-mile journey from Kut to Baghdad and eventual internment across Asia Minor were described by Major E. W. C. Sandes's *In Kut and Captivity*. Officers may have been treated with respect but the rank and file, and the Indians, were subjected to callous abuse and even the repatriated wounded were often left to struggle to their deaths in the heat without medicines or food.

More than a thousand prisoners died en route to Anatolia. The *History of the Dorsetshire Regiment, 1914-19* states:

> *'Of the 350 Dorsets who started from Kut only about 140 answered their names at the muster-roll at Bagtsche Station, where they arrived at the end of June. Moreover, when the survivors did at last arrive at their destinations they were almost without exception put to work on the railway or some similar task, and kept hard at it on the railway or some similar task, and kept hard at it on inadequate rations, under insanitary conditions, herded together in the filthiest quarters, and frequently treated with utmost brutality.'*

Field-Marshal von der Goltz never saw his victory, dying in Baghdad on 19 April, and General Townshend was privileged to see out the war from an island off Constantinople.

Intended as reinforcements for the 2nd Dorsets in Mesopotamia, the freshly-formed 3rd Battalion, Dorsetshire Regiment arrived in Basra on 6 January 1916. The draft of ten officers and 400 men had sailed in the *Kinfauns Castle* from Devonport, along with detachments of the Norfolk and Royal West Kent regiments and the Oxford Light

2ND BATTALION, DORSETSHIRE REGIMENT

Infantry. The 'Tigris Corps' played a valiant part in the failed attempts at reaching Kut. One scratch regiment was known as the 'Norsets' for its bucolic mix of two companies from the Norfolks and two of Dorsets. In July 1916 the Dorset component of the 'Norsets' was re-named the 2nd (Provisional) Battalion, Dorsetshire Regiment, in recognition of the fact that their namesakes were in captivity for the duration.

The Mesopotamian front took a year to turn towards Turkey. In taking Campbell's Bridge, a crossing of the Ruz Canal on the road to Baghdad, the battalion suffered over 220 casualties out of some 500 who took part in the action. Among the 20 men killed at Jebel Hamrin, on 25 March 1917, were Major Weldon and Lieutenant J. S. R. Hodgson. Captain W. B. Thomson, who was missing and later presumed killed, had arrived with the original contingent of 2nd Dorsets in 1914. Having been twice wounded, and invalided back home once, he had insisted on returning to the fray.

The battalion was brought back to strength by a draft of 280 men, under Lieutenant L. J. Woodhouse, who arrived from Bangalore on 11 May 1917. The advance was led by Lieutenant-General Sir Frederick Maude who died from cholera on 18 November 1917. On 12 April 1918, the Dorsets left Mesopotamia on the *Ixion*, with the 3rd (Lahore) Division, to join General Sir Edmund Allenby's victorious Egyptian Expeditionary Force in Palestine. This, unlike the adventures in Gallipoli to one side and Mesopotamia on the other, was the British success story in the Middle East and the glamorous antidote – complete with Lawrence of Arabia – to stagnation in the trenches.

In their last action of the war, during the big advance towards Lake Tiberius which started on 19 September 1918, the Dorsets in the Holy Land lost 20 men killed and missing and 61 wounded. Captain Woodhouse won the Military Cross for leading the attack. Major Clemson was similarly decorated and Lieutenant-Colonel Horace Akroyd Case was awarded the Distinguished Service Order.

2nd Dorsets' Christmas card, from Harry in Basra to Bill in Dorchester, 1918.

Damascus fell on 1 October, Beirut on the 8th, and the finale took place at Aleppo. The Dorsets saw none of it. Fast-moving Australian troops and the Arab Camel Corps went forward into the end-game, and the Lahore Division marched back to Jiljulieh, to spend the last month of the war clearing the battlefield there and at Mejdel Zaba. Then the battalion occupied post-war Damascus, for six months, during the influenza pandemic.

General Allenby's key aide was Lieutenant-General Sir Louis Bols, who progressed from commanding the 1st Battalion, Dorsetshire Regiment in France to Chief of Staff, Egyptian Expeditionary Force, in 1917. Along with Colonel T. E. Lawrence and Colonial Secretary Winston Churchill, he attended the Peace Conference in Paris in 1919, to discuss the future of the Middle East. He went back to Palestine as Military Administrator in Jerusalem before returning to England as commander of the Wessex Division of Southern Command. From 1927 he was governor of Bermuda, and died in Bath on 13 September 1930, on coming home for a colonial conference.

twelve

3rd & 4th Battalions, Dorsetshire Regiment

DORSET'S TERRITORIAL SOLDIERS – 'the old Militia' – were reorganised as the 3rd (Militia) Battalion, Dorsetshire Regiment, in 1907. It was mobilised at the Depot Barracks, Dorchester, on 5 August 1914, under the command of Lieutenant-Colonel E. C. Castleman-Smith.

The battalion was given the task of managing the mobilisation of several hundred reservists in August 1914. It was also required to defend the county's key points. One company marched to the camp at Wyke Regis, Weymouth, and another to Upton Fort, to man the coast defences protecting Portland Harbour. Detachments were to guard the waterworks at Sutton Poyntz and the Whitehead Torpedo Works at Ferrybridge. Hearing of the other two battalions and their progress, those left behind on the Dorset coast were keen to receive more ambitious marching order 'before the show was all over'.

Proving reinforcements for the front soon became a prime purpose of the battalion, and in accommodating, equipping and training young men they soon found that the War Office was liable to send them the most unlikely bands of recruits. These included several hundred miners from South Wales. Bureaucratic chaos followed due to inexperience in dealing with large numbers of men sharing the same surname and similar initials (resolved by designating them as Jones I, Jones II, Jones III and so on). Leaking canvas tents 'made even the English swear in Welsh' in the early months of the war.

The attrition rate in the other battalions was such that more than 300 officers and 6,000 other ranks passed through the 3rd Battalion, most of them via Wyke Camp and rifle-range at Chickerell, by Christmas 1916. One officer alone was responsible for taking 98 separate draft of men from Dorset to France, with the largest – 300 strong – leaving Wyke Regis on 12 May 1915, to make up losses in the 1st Battalion, Dorsetshire Regiment, during the second Battle of Ypres.

Depot Barracks of the Dorset-shire Regiment in Dorchester.

The training team at Wyke Regis also received detachments of Dragoon Guards and even a company of conscientious objectors. Non-combatant duties included the planting of rows of potatoes in allotments between the huts, using mules from the machine-gun section to work the plough.

Colonel Castleman-Smith who was succeeded by Lieutenant-Colonel V. T. Worship in 1916.

The status of the 4th Battalion, Dorsetshire Regiment, was somewhat different, as it comprised territorial units of 'citizen soldiers'. They were administered from the Territorial Forces Association office in High West Street, Dorchester, under Major Alfred Rolph Pope, who took over the Old Drill Hall in nearby Princes Street as a temporary barracks.

Dorchester recruting officer Major A. Rolph Pope.

When war was declared, the battalion happened to be together on Salisbury Plain, under canvas at their summer camp beside Sling Plantation, Bulford. On the evening of 4 August 1914 they entrained from Salisbury Station for Devonport. Their task was the defence of the western side of Plymouth Sound, from Whitesand to Mount Edgecombe. The commanding officer was Lieutenant-Colonel W. H. Baxter from Sherborne who was stationed in Penlee Battery.

On Sunday 4 August they were relieved by Worcestershire reservists, taken back to Salisbury, and marched to Durrington where they joined the 'concentrated' Wessex Division. The Dorset Territorials, who were only liable for service in the United Kingdom, then volunteered – providing the necessary two-thirds in support of the move – to go overseas. Major Pope, at their depot in Dorchester, processed new recruits who joined the battalion on Salisbury Plain. The bulk of new arrivals were without uniform.

Training was cut short by Major-General Donald who gave them the news that abroad was to be further away than France:

DORSET IN THE FIRST WORLD WAR

'You men of the Dorsetshire Regiment – your regiment bears the proud motto, "Primus in Indis". You shall be the first of the Territorials to set foot in India.'

The 1/4th Battalion landed in Bombay on 10 November 1914. It frequently provided drafts to fighting, notably 25 men under Captain C. W. Symes who were transferred to the 2nd Battalion of the Dorsets in time for the siege at Kut and, for most of them, death in captivity. Captain Symes, a typical territorial, had been Blandford's Town Clerk. The remainder of the 1/4th Dorsets sailed for Mesopotamia on the British-India transport *Elephanta* on 15 February 1916. They landed at Fao, at the mouth of the Shatt-el-Arab waterway on the 23rd, and took part in the determined – but abortive – attempts to relieve the forces trapped in Kut.

The 2/4th Battalion, another 'Home-Service' reserve unit, sailed from Southampton for India in the *Ionian* on 12 December 1914 under Lieutenant-Colonel F. W. Scott. For much of the time the 2/4th's primary purpose was to provide drafts for the 1/4th Battalion. The best known 2/4th volunteer was the impresario George Hay who organised concerts for the battalion at Jullundur. In April and May 1917 the battalion had a proper duty, guarding the 'Gateway of India' at the port of Bombay. The General Officer Commanding was impressed by their sobriety:

'During this period no cases of drunkenness or indiscipline amongst any of the ranks has occurred, and such exemplary conduct in a city like Bombay is, I consider, worthy of mention.'

In September 1917, the 2/4ths joined the 75th Division in the Egyptian Expeditionary Force and were sent to Wadi Ghuzzeh, near Gaza. Their first casualty, Private W. Legg, was killed by shrapnel in the trenches on the 27th. The Battle of Gaza was fought in the first week of November. The Dorsets held the front line salient after the Turks were ousted from Beersheba and abandoned Sheria. There was nearly an 'unfortunate incident' – showing the military imperative of standard English – when a 'supposed patrol of "Turks"' was in reality a patrol of "Ghurks".'

The 2/4th went on to play a part in securing the strategic Junction Station and Nabi Samweil. The latter was the 'Key to Jerusalem' which duly fell on 9 December 1917. Rain then stopped the war and the regiment spent Christmas at Bidieh in the Judaean Hills. They found the telephone had been disconnected to a neighbouring unit, to uproarious laughter from the Australians concerned, as 'the wires had been cut intentionally in order that the festive season might be kept in good old Australian style, without risk of disturbance'.

The most difficult action was to storm the deep-cut gorge known as Wadi Deir Ballut on 12 March 1918 though casualties were light. Two men were killed and six wounded. Moving forward in April to Three Bushes Hill at Berukin, which remained closely fought from the 9th through to the 13th, was much more costly. A hundred men were killed, wounded or taken prisoner. The losses included Lieutenant W. H. R. Crick who had been accepted by Magdalen College, Oxford, on leaving Lancing College at Easter in 1915. Instead he joined the 2/4th in India. Another clergyman's son, Lieutenant W. R. Powell who had also chosen India over Oxford, 'died cheering on his men when they were hard pressed and the situation was looking critical'.

The 2/4th Battalion was disbanded in August 1918. Because of the situation on the Western Front, no further reinforcements were being sent to Palestine and the only way General Allenby could keep his key regiments up to strength was by drafting men from second line territorial units which ceased to exist.

There was also a 3/4th Battalion of the county regiment, which moved from Bath to Winton, Bournemouth, in spring 1915. It was commanded by Lieutenant-Colonel H. A. Cartwright, with Major R. W. Dickinson as his second in command. They moved to Romsey in 1916 where Cartwright was succeeded by Lieutenant-Colonel J. R. Wyatt. The battalion became a convalescence unit, for those recovering from active service, and received many of its fresh recruits from the Channel Islands. These were busily trained and sent overseas. In October 1916, the battalion returned to Bournemouth, to billets at Queen's Park and Boscombe. In the spring of 1917 it joined the 33rd Training Reserve at Sutton Veny, near Warminster, and was upgraded to an Officers' Training Corps.

A year later, under Major D. C. Greenlees, the 3/4th Battalion went to Northern Ireland, with the Wessex Reserve Brigade. To a writer in the *History of the Dorsetshire Regiment, 1914-19*, this was good news:

'From Rose to Frank', serving at the time in Rochester, Kent.

> *'In view of the general unrest in Ireland, life was more thrilling than on Salisbury Plain. Conditions were almost equivalent to those of active service, or the Indian Frontier. For example, rifles had to be carefully protected, constantly checked, and carried on all duties, including church parades. An incident is recorded that happened about this time, which illustrates the strained relationships then existing.*

> *'A German submarine attacked, torpedoed, and sank a large liner in the vicinity. The shipwrecked, rescued crew were brought into Ebrington Barracks. The submarine was then captured, her crew being taken alive, and brought into Londonderry as prisoners. The shipwrecked sailors turned out in force and attacked the Germans, who were only saved by their escort from having an extremely rough handling. This caused the local Sinn Feiners to attack the shipwrecked sailors. Thereupon the local Orangemen retaliated by attacking the Sinn Feiners. At this stage the Dorsets were called out to keep order. The day concluded with a fight between the Sinn Feiners and American sailors stationed in the neighbourhood.'*

That winter an outbreak of septic pneumonia joined the influenza pandemic in taking a disproportionate toll of the fit and the young. Among those who died was the 3/4th's Quartermaster, Captain J. Hoskins, 'an outstanding personality, and popular with all ranks' whose body was brought back from Londonderry to Dorchester for burial. The battalion continued to serve in Northern Ireland after the Armistice, and grew in strength to 1,800, through the enlistment 'of youths just eligible for service'. The 3rd Battalion, Dorsetshire Regiment was then transferred to Ebrington Barracks from

Wyke Regis, in the spring of 1919, and the 3/4th Dorsets moved to huts in Clooney Park on the outskirts of Derry. The 3/4th Battalion was disbanded on 17 June 1919 when Lieutenant-Colonel Hugh Thurston gave up command. Its remaining responsibilities passed to the 1st Dorsets.

Those who came forward for military service but were too old or unsuitable for sending overseas found themselves in the Dorset Volunteers which guarded the coast and strategic installations. 'Entrenching' became its main task as volunteers were regarded as 'the last ditchers' at a time when regular units were preoccupied with sustaining the overseas war.

In 1917, under Lieutenant-Colonel C. P. W. Kindersley-Porcher, the force was recognised by the War Office, and designated the Dorsetshire Volunteer Regiment. In August 1918 it was re-named the 1st Volunteer Battalion, Dorsetshire Regiment. Headquarters were in Dorchester and detachments were formed there, in the county town, and at Blandford, Branksome, Bridport, Charmouth, Gillingham, Lyme Regis, Poole, Portland, Sherborne, Sturminster Newton, Wareham, West Moors and Weymouth. All were required to carry out 15 mandatory monthly drills. Most recruits had regular work so inter-detachment field days generally took place on Sundays.

The most over-stretched single month of the war – causing an emergency throughout the Army – was in March 1918 when the German advanced forced back Allied lines on the Western Front. In August 1918 the month was devoted to field training from Trigon Camp at Wareham. At the Armistice all activities and parades ceased, apart from Sunday church services, and the Volunteers were first to begin the process of 'fading away'. Their unit was formally disbanded on 6 March 1920.

thirteen

5th Battalion, Dorsetshire Regiment

THE 5TH BATTALION of the county regiment was among the 80 'K1' service units formed by Lord Kitchener as his 'First New Army' on becoming Secretary of State for War. Dorchester was so overcrowded with recruits by the end of August 1914 that the battalion was transferred to Grantham, Lincolnshire, where it was adopted by the 3rd Earl of Brownlow at Belton House and given the run of an estate that extended to 58,400 acres. The Machine Gun Corps was formed there in 1915.

In April 1915, the new Dorsets (nicknamed 'All Saints' as they had been so well behaved) moved south with the 11th Division to Witley Camp, Hindhead, Surrey. Lord Kitchener came down on 5 May to watch an attack on Brook and Albury, and King George V on the 31st for a big review on Hankley Common. They were to sail from Liverpool at 14.00 on 3 July 1915, under Lieutenant-Colonel C. C. Hannay, to join the Mediterranean Expeditionary Force which was heading for Gallipoli.

Six battalions embarked on the 50,000-ton Cunard liner *Aquitania*, escorted by two destroyers, as protection against submarines. They passed through the dangerous waters off Cornwall during darkness and parted with the destroyers 100 miles west of the Scillies, though this proved premature as one U-boat did fire a torpedo (which missed) and they spotted a submarine on the surface the following morning. The ship, which made 23 knots, anchored amid a great fleet in the harbour at Lemnos on 10 July.

The 5th Dorsets belonged to the first wave of Lord Kitchener's 'New Army'.

The men disembarked to bivouac on the 11th and transferred to Imbros on the 19th. Fatigues in the dust, described as 'coolie work', were blamed for outbreaks of diarrhoea. It was decided that the 11th Division would land at Nibrunesi Point, at the south end of Suvla Bay, to take pressure off the Anzac positions – those of the Australian and New Zealand Army Corps. Three days' rations had been issued on 5 August and troop-carrying motor-lighters headed for the shore at 22.30 on the 6th. Most of the men followed in row-boats. Heavy Turkish artillery later in the night caused all shipping to be cleared from the bay with the result that the battalion was 100 men short as it started operations on the 7th.

5th Dorsets camped at Belton House, Lincolnshire, early in 1915.

Lieutenant Lloyd was killed early in the day, and Lieutenants Cooke and Derry wounded, but the biggest lost was the Adjutant, Captain Carruthers-Little, who was shot through the heart. The battalion had taken its objective at Karakol Dagh, otherwise known as Hill 28, and was then told to cover the flank for the next attack, on Chocolate Hill. Detachments led by Major Leslie and Captain H. N. le Marchant met on the hill on 8 August. A total of 14 men had been killed and 60 wounded. Little water, and no other rations, had arrived to alleviate the heat exhaustion.

The plan for the 9th was for the 11th Division to seize Scimitar Hill and Ismail Oglu Tepe on the ridge east of Yilghin Burnu. Making progress through the spiky scrub became increasingly difficult for men fatigued by chronic thirst. Captain le Marchant was killed and Major Weldon seriously wounded, both being hit when they were recklessly assessing the deteriorating situation. Nineteen other men had been killed, a dozen were missing, and more than 60 were wounded. It was all for nothing as neither objective had been taken and units on each side were falling back. The 5th Dorsets had to conform. The exceptions were two detachments, one under Captain Vincent and Lieutenant Sanders, and the other under Second-Lieutenant F. Smith, who held their forward positions (and even found a spring which made the situation worth defending). The men had to be ordered back on the 10th, after which the battalion was relieved by the Inniskilling Fusiliers on the 11th, and withdrew to Lala Baba.

The Commander-in-Chief, General Sir Ian Hamilton, was determined to make a final effort on Scimitar Hill and Ismail Oglu Tepe. On August 13 the Dorsets went into support trenches and then advanced to a farm known as Dead Man's House, as they edged around Hetman Chair and the happily named Valley of Death. None of the officers who reached the Turkish lines returned. Major Leslie was among the dead. A total of 25 men were known to have been killed, nearly 200 were missing, and 90 wounded had been recovered.

The battalion, like many others, had been so seriously savaged that its remnants were merged (with the 11th Manchesters) into a composite 'No. 2 Battalion'. They were moved to the Karakol Dagh section of the line where they faced a 500-feet 'razor-backed slope' and had to hunker down in the rocks. Extreme heat gave way to severe cold, bringing a blizzard, and harassment and shell-fire had to be endured while an evacuation was planned.

On 20 December 1915 the battalion embarked on HMT *Abbasieh*, from Suvla for Imbros, but had to return to harbour after she had collided with a tramp-steamer and twisted her bows. Another transport took them to Imbros the following day. On 27 January 1916, the 5th Battalion boarded the *Seang Bee* for Alexandria, arriving on 1 February. From there they moved to El Ferdan on the Suez Canal. The next posting, on 3 July 1916, was from Alexandria to France on the HMT *Transylvania*.

The battalion disembarked in Marseilles on 11 July and arrived by train in St Pol on the 14th. The 11th Division was moving forward to Wailly in a 'quiet sector' south of Arras. Battalion strength was 43 officers and 861 men. On 7 September they moved forward to 'the maze of trenches south of Thiepval'. Taking an immense dug-out beneath Mouquet Farm cost the 7th Battalion 15 men killed or missing and 40 wounded, but the Germans had many more casualties, who they were allowed to remove under a Red Cross flag.

After resting at Albert and Englebelmer, the battalion went back to the front on 26 September, to face the formidable Stuff Redoubt at Grandcourt. This was reached in an offensive on the 27th but the Germans drove them back in a counter-attack. Colonel Hannay moved his headquarters forward despite a shell-fire barrage described by one officer as 'the worst I ever saw in the war'. They dug in beside the secondary target, Zollern Redoubt, which was abandoned apart from the dead and wounded. The battalion chaplain features in the regimental history, as Revd F. R. Barry:

'*... went from shell-hole to shell-hole, searching for wounded, binding up their wounds and guiding the stretcher-bearers to them. The German shelling was*

8 Platoon, B-Company, of the 5th Battalion, Dorsetshire Regiment.

very heavy and it was a marvel that this errand of mercy did not cost him his life.'

He won the Distinguished Service Order though the men thought it worthy of a VC. Of the 600 who had gone into action, 62 were killed, 60 missing, and 230 wounded. The situation with the missing, however, was unusually encouraging as they had dispersed into German positions. As a reward, for a day that had gone remarkably well, the 11th Division was given six weeks out of the line, in rest, recuperation and training at Domqueur. Replacement drafts included nearly 200 men from the North Somerset Yeomanry. The 5th Battalion's full strength swelled to 35 officers and 1,111 men.

Burial of two British soldiers on the battlefield.

In the first week of January, 1917, the battalion had five men killed and a dozen wounded from shell-fire as they prepared to attack from Beaucourt. They moved up to the front line after dark on the 10th with 'zero' being 06.40 on the 11th. Things started badly, in dense fog and a snow storm, as D-Company advanced on a chalk-pit. Hordes of Germans emerged from an undetected dug-out. A pitched battle ensued, leaving the company cut-off in an untenable position. Second-Lieutenant E. A. Shephard and 25 men were killed; Second-Lieutenants Bateman and Kelley and 90 missing; and Second-Lieutenants Straughan and Wanstall and 50 men wounded. If it was any consolation, they received a mention in Sir Douglas Haig's next despatch, for having carried out a diversion that took the enemy's attention off the successful main attack by the 91st Brigade.

It was the 11th Division's last experience of the Somme. On 19 January 1917 it was relieved by the Royal Naval Division. Activities progressed from soldiering to navvying after 16 March, being dedicated to road building after the Germans retreated to the Hindenburg Line. They returned to the war at Bapaume and had 8 killed and 21 wounded when a couple of stray shells landed among men and mules (killing four animals). They were under orders to move to Flanders for the attack at Messines on 7 June. In the event the battalion was not called on and stayed in reserve but found itself regularly strafed as it dug two communication trenches from the Mauve Line to the new front line.

The long-expected third Battle of Ypres coincided with the constant rains of August and continuous downpours of September which turned it into the muddiest of the Great War. The *History of the Dorsetshire Regiment, 1914-19* records:

5TH BATTALION, DORSETSHIRE REGIMENT

'By October, as the 5th Dorsets were to find, the ground was a mere morass, in which movement was always slow and difficult, and the troops in the fighting line suffered such tremendous hardships that the memories of that autumn are a veritable nightmare.'

Gas-shelling remained a threat and night bombing from aeroplanes was 'a most unpleasant new development'. At 04.45 on 15 August 1917 'a splendid barrage crashed down' and Lewis guns opened up on Maison Bulgare and other enemy strong-points as the 5th Battalion rushed forwards. The men tried to keep pace with the barrage which advanced at the rate of 100 yards every five minutes. Second-Lieutenant Statham's B-Company platoon took two field-guns and 60 prisoners from one strong-point. Captain Wiltshire, though wounded, also cleared pillboxes and took prisoners, as the platoons reached their objective by crossing the Langemarck-Winnnipeg road. C-Company had strayed over the divisional boundary to take Alouette Farm. The Dorsets, who had captured more than 200 prisoners, were relieved by the Sherwood Foresters on the 17th.

Second-Lieutenant A. R. Ball and 25 men were killed, 4 missing, and 117 wounded – making a casualty toll below 150 – compared with losses of more than a thousand in the three other battalions of the 34th Brigade that took part. They pulled back to the relative safety of Siege Camp which was nearly punctured for Major Burrows and Captain James when an 8-inch shell left a crater on the site of their tent. The officers were out at the time. Then the brigade moved back to Dirty Bucket Camp, near Poperinghe, and other reserve positions. Corporal Riach was killed, and several men wounded, in an accident during grenade practice.

The Dorsets returned to the line by bus from Herzelle on the evening of 2 October. They were delivered to Dirty Bucket Camp for the familiar march to Siege Camp. The attack was planned for 15.00 on 4 October. Battalion headquarters was shifted forward across 'a mass of shell-holes' to Bulow Farm. Elsewhere, however, the line had not budged, so the order was given to retreat to the old lines from positions regarded as indefensible. Captain A. C. Dancer MC had been killed, among more than 60 casualties in the 5th Battalion, with nothing to show for it.

On the evening of 5 October 1917, the Dorsets relieved the Manchesters and took charge of the front line at Bavaroise Farm and Gloster Farm. Captain G. Stockwell was

Electrocuted German infantrymen.

*In October 1917 the 5th
Dorsets were in mining villages
beside the ruins of Lens.*

*In October 1917 the 5th
Dorsets were in mining villages
beside the ruins of Lens.*

killed before the 'unhealthy' headquarters were transferred to nearby shell-holes.
Artillery and sniper fire were taking a toll. By the time it was relieved, later in the
week, the battalion had 30 men killed, 14 missing, and 120 wounded.

This time, from Dirty Bucket Camp, the 11th Division were taken by train to Serques,
and then to Moulle, before setting off on 18 October to relieve the 6th Division in the
Loos salient, in mining villages near Lens. Captain D. Lindsey was killed – while
venturing into no man's land to try and ambush some Germans – but otherwise the
battalion had a quiet mid-winter with a total of four men dead and 15 wounded.
All that changed after a move to Philosophe and its working coalpit on 24 January
1918. A seven-month routine followed of '16 days in and 8 days out'. The defences
were frequently tested with trench-mortars, snipers and hostile patrols, during a 'lively'
February which culminated in a frontal attack, successfully fought off on the 27th.
On 21 March a raid on Border Redoubt was repelled by A-Company. This preceded
the 'Boche push' at Lys – 'Hun' was the other epithet for German – which caused the
immediate cancellation of all leave. This was particular sad for Major Burrows, who
was never able to take his promised 'war-weary' month before he was gassed. On
that occasion, at dinner, the headquarters' waiter continued to serve soup with
streaming eyes as he whispered to the Commanding Officer:

> *'Excuse me, Sir, I think there is gas about.'*

The chaplain, Revd. W. H. Kay, was killed while he stood outside battalion headquarters. Colonel Hannay left the battalion, on his own feet, as he was promoted to
command the 75th Brigade. He was replaced by Major C. S. Worthington who was
promoted Lieutenant-Colonel.

On 6 August 1918, on taking over the Hulluch sector, Captain Russell led B-Company
on a raid at 14.15 against German trenches near Bois Hugo. Thirty Germans were
killed, and more ran away, for the loss of two dead, one missing and 16 wounded. By
14.30, as the Germans shelled their own lines, the raid was over and Captain Russell
was rewarded with a Military Cross. Sergeants Barker and Wright, Corporal Jennings,
and Private Squires, each received the Military Medal.

On 1 October a renewed German attack was successfully held. Lance-Corporal Vallence distinguished himself by coming back to battalion headquarters with two prisoners, when he met six Germans. He shot two and the other four immediately surrendered. Then two more Germans approached. Vallence killed one and the other ran away. Having reached headquarters with his six captives, he was awarded the Distinguished Conduct Medal.

Battalion losses were heavy, however, with Second-Lieutenant W. J. K. Vincent and 50 men being killed or missing. Five officers and 209 other ranks were wounded.

On 3 October an unlucky shell seriously wounded Lieutenant-Colonel Worthington – who died from his injuries on the 14th – and killed the chaplain, Revd E. O. Read, with four stretcher-bearers, and the Medical Officer, Captain Cooper. Major T. H. Owen took over the battalion which had few more shots to fire. The division was behind the line, beyond Bavai, when the *Battalion Diary* records the Armistice celebrations:

> *'The band at once fell in and paraded up and down the main road, the whole battalion falling in behind it as it passed by. Popular airs were played and then the officers took over the band instruments, headed by the Quartermaster. The column then marched back down the road. At 11 a.m. the battalion paraded and were addressed by the Commanding Officer, who especially mentioned the day as being the anniversary of "Sarah Sands" Day. In the afternoon impromptu sports were arranged, free beer being issued to the men.'*

The battalion began demobilising at Denain, on the Scheldt Canal – though there were only a few miners to qualify as the first returnees on 2 January 1919 – and the process continued for several months, until the 5th Battalion was disbanded back in Dorchester.

fourteen

6th Battalion, Dorsetshire Regiment

TWELVE THOUSAND MEN of the 17th Division, from both sides of the Pennines, were ordered south by the War Office, into tents at Worgret Camp, Wareham. They were joined at Wareham by a hastily formed 6th (Service) Battalion, Dorsetshire Regiment, under Lieutenant-Colonel Cecil Alured Rowley DSO (won in South Africa). The battalion was formed at the Depot Barracks, Dorchester, on 6 September and left by train for Wareham on 18 August 1914. The regimental history records:

> *'Every man was a volunteer, one of Kitchener's second 100,000.'*

Its assets included Company Sergeant Major J. 'Old Mac' Macmullen who was leader of the band and had secured the county's best collection of instruments. He started the day with the regimental march and always ensured a stirring return to camp. The top three popular songs were 'Tipperary', 'At the halt on the left form Platoon' and 'Hold your hand out, you naughty boy'. The haunting refrain of 'The Long, Long Trail' became the battle song of the Somme.

Three hundred of the thousand men came from Dorset, and were concentrated in D-Company. The northerners led the banter with dialect-imitating cries such as:

> *'Be I Darzet ... Where be to?'*

The Adjutant, Lieutenant T. S. Rendall, had been 'stolen' from the 2nd Dorsets. Seven majors were brought out of retirement. Two, Major H. Welman and Major D. Hughes-Onslow, went with the men into active service, but others could be a liability. Major Hammond was found to suffer 'natural blindness' after losing his way on night operations, and credited with this exchange with the Commanding Officer:

> *Rowley – 'Hullo, Hammond, you haven't brushed your hair this morning.'*

Hammond – 'Damn my servant!'

Worgret Camp, Wareham, in the snow.

They each had a lively sense of humour. Colonel Rowley told how he was challenged by a sentry who emerged from behind a gorse bush:

'Advance and be baptised.'

Life at Wareham, often wet and windy, prepared the men for the privations of France. In an average week they covered a hundred miles on foot. Trenches were dug across the knoll beside Seven Barrows, at Coldharbour, where Major Welman emphasised the necessity for 'wavy lines' as a precaution against air attack, artillery range-finding, or the enemy firing a machine-gun along the length of the trench. A rifle-range was constructed across Hyde Heath. Major-General Thomas Pilcher, General Officer Commanding the 17th Division, lectured officers on trench warfare in Wareham Cinema. Bathing took place in the River Piddle and a regimental dinner was held on the beach at Arish Mell, on 8 April 1915.

They left Wareham for Romsey on 27 May 1915, and then marched back to Dorset in a 50-mile walk to Canford Park, followed by bivouac camps across the New Forest and a shooting course at Fovant. Captain G. O'Hanlon described the day of full mobilisation, on 7 July:

> *'Final inspections were held; identity discs were issued; pay-books and wills witnessed: even the dullest was forced to realise the nearer chances of sudden death. On the 12th an advanced party of three officers and 96 other ranks left with all the transport for Southampton and Havre. On the following day the Commanding Officer gave an address, and then with the band really giving tongue, and flags flying and men singing (not all the same song) the battalion marched bravely to Romsey Station and entrained for Folkestone*

and the unknown beyond. Under the gas-lamps of Guildford Station the band of the queen's played the regimental march, and a hysterical girl did her best to embrace the embarrassed colonel. Thirty officers and 990 men were on the roll.'

The *St Cecilia* and two destroyers crossed 'a phosphorescent sea' to Boulogne where they docked at 03.00 on 14 July. A march, in sweltering heat, and 'a train of cattle-trucks' took them to Lumbres, west of St Omer, in the vicinity of Ypres. General Pilcher complimented Colonel Rowley on having:

'... the most highly disciplined battalion of the 17th Division.'

The first man to be killed was Private A. J. Banks of A-Company, from Cattistock, on 25 July 1915. Most of the losses were to random artillery shells. During a marching back to the line, from Reninghelst, one of the men spoilt General Pilcher's high opinion of the battalion, when he was asked to hand over his gas-kit for a demonstration, 'only to discover a pair of dirty socks'.

Lieutenant A. E. Broad carried out a daring one-man reconnaissance on 15 September. He passed undetected through the German lines, avoiding booby traps and listening to conversations, and then lobbed a jam-tin bomb into a crater as a leaving present. He returned, soaked and muddy, to win the battalion's first Military Cross.

Lieutenant C. K. Homan, remembered as 'the beloved "babe" of the battalion' was shot by a sniper on the 18th. Six men were killed and 43 wounded during this tour of the front before they went back to Steenvoorde for training 'in bombing and Lewis-gun work'.

Their next lines were at Hooge and included a crater which had been left by a huge mine. Captain O'Hanlon contributed some of the most descriptive passages to the regimental history:

'The hellish crater blown up on June 16th was half full of water; its shiny surface bubbled with the gases from putrefying corpses below. The living jostled by the protruding limbs of decomposing dead. Other corpses lay unburied in no man's land, and their rotting flesh reflected in the moonlight an iridescent green. You could pick up a derelict boot and find it full, or study at ease the anatomy of the human skull.

'Communication trenches collapsed in the rain: and rain fell on 47 days between July 14th and November 30th. Thigh-boots were issued in the dark in the Ypres barracks, and boot wardens were invented, but nothing could keep out the wet, and the agonies of trench foot began.'

The 6th Battalion was in reserve at the time of the German advance down from the Bluff, on 12 February 1916, when after mine explosions and intense bombardment the enemy took 500 yards of canal-side trench from the 51st Brigade. On the 15th, 'in darkness, with sleet falling', the Dorsets left Dickebusch, for Spoil Bank headquarters and a counter-attack beside the canal. They found themselves in 'a mysterious new trench' and advanced towards the Bluff. Major Hughes-Onslow was wounded. Later that night, after Captain E. C. B. Blencowe of A-Company was shot through the heart, Private Follett from A-Company took the initiative, telling the men:

'All the NCOs are down. Follow me, boys, we must beat them.'

He then attacked a German with his bayonet. Follett was awarded the Distinguished Conduct Medal. Lieutenant A. E. Broad of the bombing squad was fatally injured. At 04.30 on the 16th, after 20 hours endurance, the Commanding Officer ordered the withdrawal. Forty men were dead and a hundred wounded had to be brought in, though there might have been more, but for the recent introduction of steel helmets. Sergeant Buckley led the rescue and gained the DCM and a mention in despatches.

On 13 March the battalion left Belgium, for the comparative peace of trenches defending the River Lys in France, but its day of destiny was being planned. Though they were held in reserve when the great Battle of the Somme opened on 1 July 1916, at 17.30 they were ordered forward as the offensive collapsed. Fortunately there was a change of mind, Captain O'Hanlon records with obvious relief:

'At the last moment the order was cancelled, and the Dorsets were saved from the holocaust.'

The men spent the night around the cemetery at Fricourt. They suffered in a bombardment on 6 July, during which Captain G. H. Penney was deafened and had to hand over D-Company to Captain C. H. L. Kindersley from Tincleton. Lieutenant Llewellyn, waking up from a faint in a dug-out in Bottom Wood, 'hearing Welsh and seeing bright lights, thought he was in Hell'.

Emerging from that wood, once delightful with honeysuckle and wild strawberries, Second-Lieutenants K. H. Moore and G. C. Goodall were killed, as they attacked nearby Strip Trench on the 7th. Private Cunningham (awarded the DCM) dressed the wounds of Major T. H. F. Johnson (awarded the DSO) under fire, and took three hours to drag him back. Private Harris (awarded the Military Medal), though wounded in five places, insisted on bringing an injured comrade back to the wood. Despite the casualties, C-Company succeeded in securing most of Wood Trench by 09.15, with a haul of 50 rifles and hundreds of stick-bombs.

In a dash against a German position, Lieutenant G. L. Davidson (awarded the Military Cross) was fatally wounded. Lieutenant W. S. A. Clarke was killed while leading a patrol into Mametz Wood on 10 July. Major Hughes-Onslow was killed by a sniper, from a tree, while in Wood Trench. He had already been hit in the hand, earlier in the day, but hid the wound with a glove. Company Sergeant-Major Franklin (awarded the DCM) spotted and shot the German. 6th Battalion casualties totalled 58 dead and 90 wounded; 'by good luck the smallest casualties in the brigade'. D-Company brought back a drum, as their trophy, from the Triangle.

On 13 July, Major-General P. R. Robertson CMG took over divisional command. The

Dorsets were rested behind the line, excused all fatigues, in tents at Dernancourt, from where they moved to Belle Vue Farm, and trenches near Longueval in August, with headquarters in a dug-out that was one positive gain from the Somme offensive. Entrenching followed – the appropriately named Dorset Trench across high ground – with losses including Lance-Corporal Fry and Lieutenant R. D'Albertanson, who died before he knew he had been awarded the Military Cross for his previous month's efforts.

Return to Belle Vue Farm was remembered for delousing 'with the aid of hot flat-irons'. From 'inhospitable billets' at Sailly-au-Bois, after the 20th, they used gas-masks – box respirators – to mount raids for honey. Private Cobb from Buckland Newton perfected his own rat-trap with which he caught more than 60 on one tour in the trenches. The rest of the summer was marked by much marching marred by 'the decrepit state of boots and the impossibility of procuring new ones. Lieutenant E. K. A. Boyce, asked by divisional headquarters to cross no man's land and bring back a sample of the enemy wire, provided two envelopes in response:

> *'On the first he wrote – "Herewith sample of wire". On the other – "Herewith sample of gap".'*

The second envelope was empty. Later, Captain O'Hanlon writes, he bore his wounds with stoic fortitude:

> *'I have just had my twelfth operation. When I get an artificial limb I shall be a formidable person. Imagine hitting a Boche between the eyes with a wooden fist.'*

On 28 October, from Mansel Camp – its only virtue being the Dorset family name – the battalion headed 'for the muck by Trones Wood'. The Germans seemed to know a relief was in progress, judging from their shelling, and there was no proper hand-over by guides from the previous unit:

> *'The shelling was as persistent as the rain. There were no communications trenches, and runners by day had to risk the open. The trenches themselves were ill-defined and full of liquid mud which clung. If a man stuck he could not be dug out or pulled out – he had to be scooped out by hand.'*

Both sides could be confused by the geography. One British rations party attempted returning via German trenches, and a German soldier literally fell into Zenith Trench:

> *'He was remarkably clean, "a good Catholic, and the father of many children" – one of the sort Colonel Campbell of the Bayonet School said should be killed at once. One of the men gave him a cigarette, saying: "Hullo, Alleyman; compris Verdun?"'*

Lieutenant A. Agelasto and 14 men were killed, 52 wounded, and 146 from the battalion immobilised by trench-foot, in the course of two tours. From September 'The Duds' concert party entertained companies of men twice nightly. The 6th

6TH BATTALION, DORSETSHIRE REGIMENT

Battalion recuperated at Molliens-Vidames from mid-November till 14 December. Colonel Rowley retired as Commanding Officer and was replaced by Major G. B. de M. Mairis, from India. Then Lieutenant-Colonel A. L. Moulton-Barrett took over on 8 January 1917. The battalion was over-wintering at Bronfay Camp and in the line at Sailly-Saillisel, in former German trenches that had been recently taken by the Yorkshires and literally faced the wrong way. In March they moved to Montenescourt which became the final concentration point for the Battle of Arras.

In this, on the night of 10 April, the battalion found refuge in the cellars of the Grande Place. Then on the 11th they were ordered to relieve trenches reached by the sunken road south of Fampoux. They were to head for a marsh beside the River Scarfe at Roeux. Lance-Corporal Mozley reached the objective an sent a lonely, laconic message:

> '*Can find only ten men of D-Company. No officers, only one other Lane-Corporal. Am in bottom by the marsh.*'

It was to no avail, as the left flank was exposed, and they had to come back at 23.00 hours on the 12th. Second-Lieutenant E. G. Goodman and Sergeant J. Briers, last seen together on the skyline, were presumed to have been blown up by a shell as no trace of them could be found. Captain F. W. Sprang and Second-Lieutenants L. T. Lemon and L. H. Shave were also killed. There were 84 casualties, including many wounded who were lying where they fell and had to be gathered in during the night.

On 23 April, in support of an attack on Orange Hill, the battalion was ordered to withdraw after it had dug in. Things had not been helped by an 'unfortunate misunderstanding' which caused a barrage to be mis-timed by half an hour. There was a general lack of co-ordination and a total of 110 men were listed killed, missing or wounded, for no gain whatever. Lieutenant Holt won the Military Cross for remaining with the first wave when he was the only officer left. He delayed reporting his own injuries for 24 hours.

After moving to Sombrin, the battalion was back at Arras on 2 May, where they enjoyed a boxing tournament on the 4th, until a discarded match-end set fire to rubbish and an ammunition dump. They went back into the line at Scarpe where 'C' and D-Companies took Crow and Crook Trenches on the 11th, with the loss of four killed, two missing, and 13 walking wounded. Captain A. E. Barton, in command of the battalion, heard of his promotion to Major at 15.15 hours, 'a pleasant courtesy of brigade headquarters, in the midst of preparing for a battle'. It was a bloody fight, in which D-Company alone killed 38 Germans with the bayonet. Corporal Riggs took the flank with a Lewis gun balanced in his arms. The operation was concluded at 04.30 on 12 May. One of a score of enemy prisoners volunteered the encouraging information that they had received no rations or water during the day, nor any backing from their reserve, or the artillery support they requested.

Unexpected shell-fire, however, could claim victims at any time. Major Barton was killed, and the Adjutant, Lieutenant A. H. Mitchell, wounded, as they walked along the front line at noon on 24 May. Mustard-gas shells were another occasional hazard.

Holding the front line during a night attack.

Repelling a Night Attack.

Holding the front line during a night attack.

The battalion moved to Grenas on the 28th and inducted a draft of ten officers and 260 men as reinforcements during June.

Back on the line, largely rationalising the trenches during a quiet period, death claimed another crop of men by 10 August when Lieutenant-Colonel Moulton-Barrett returned to the battalion. Eighteen men were killed and four officers and 44 other ranks wounded. Only Captain Green and Lieutenant F. J. Cummins remained from the original set of officers who left for France from Worgret Camp.

On 5 October 1917 the 17th Division marched north, to Poelcappelle, to participate in the phenomenally muddy Battle of Passchendaele. The battalion was in support during one large divisional attack which was described as 'a magnificent performance under awful conditions'. They held Gravel Farm, Tranquille Farm (a misnomer), and Olga House which was battalion headquarters. One of the problems was passing messages, as runners 'seldom arrived safely', and even with the best managed pigeon-post it took on average 25 minutes between sending the alarm and the artillery opening fire. Once the emergency was over, soup, tea and rum were served beside the Yser Canal.

From 22 October to 6 November the battalion rested at Nielles-les-Ardres. Two more tours were made during the third Battle of Ypres. Though they spent only a week in the line, and a further week in support, the attrition rate was high with three officers and 16 men killed, two men missing, and a total of 207 wounded. In one freak death a man was killed by the mess-tin from which he was drinking being jammed into his face by an explosion. Most casualties were caused by heavy artillery shells, air-dropped bombs and gas attacks. Substantial numbers of transport horses were also killed and injured.

On 5 December's the death toll included Sergeant H. N. Hansen who grew up in Schleswig-Holstein where 'as a child he had been made to kneel on the German flag and kiss it'. He had no German allegiance and joined the 6th Battalion from Singapore under the assumed name Anderson. When his origins came to light, as he was about to marry, he was threatened with court-martial but more enlightened minds put him to work interrogating prisoners after the Battle of the Somme.

The battalion quit the sector on 7 December and spent Christmas at Bertincourt. The next set of tours on the front began at Flesquieres on the 27th. It was a waiting game, as a 'tremendous' German attack was expected, though the casualty list for the next couple of months was light, at five dead and 28 wounded (though 190 were withdrawn sick). The 'Emperor's Battle' reached the 17th Division on 21 March. Their positions at Hermies were held, despite continuous bombardment, but a 'retirement' was ordered at 22.30. Ammunition and stores were destroyed. The next defences were also held but the battalion was ordered to withdraw at noon on the 23rd from Lurgan Switch to Barastre and Rocquigny.

When they passed through Beaulencourt on the 24th, the huts of the camp there were on fire, and C-Company struck off on its own. The remainder of the battalion made for Gueudecourt where two 18-pounder guns were being fired 'at top speed on the enemy'. Germans were now on three sides and the men were forced to turn north-west to Eaucourt l'Abbaye which they entered at midnight.

On the 25th a machine-gun battle broke out at dawn, killing Lieutenant R. Graham-King and wounding Lieutenant-Colonel Mairis and Lieutenant E. L. B. Lart, the battalion intelligence officer. Major 'Freddy' Morley took command. They were running short of ammunition and embarked on a series of 'rushes' from one ridge to another until they were re-united with a disparate group from the 17th Division which became known as Colonel James's Force.

Major Morley was wounded when they reached the old Somme line at Le Sars:

> *'Fancy being hit like this, and I didn't have a shave this morning.*

He was carried out on a stretcher formed from rifles and duck-boards but died later from his wounds. Colonel James's Force waded across the River Ancre, found some biscuits and onions in Miraumont, and reached a rations dump at Englebelmer on the 26th. At Forceville they linked up with some units from the division, and received Lewis gun magazines from the limbers. On 27 March 1918, after a zig-zag route of 25 miles, they reached Senlis as Captain P. S. Barber reorganised the remnants of 50th Brigade at Meaulte.

Meanwhile, Captain Llewellyn, the brigade's Staff Captain, had retreated via Rocquigny where, despite its huge red crosses, the hospital was bombed by German aircraft. The battalions split as they moved towards Le Sars and it was an exhausted contingent of Dorsets who shuffled into Fricourt:

> *'With swollen lips and blood-shot eyes they staggered on, still with a voice and a ear for a joke. The first Dorset man to meet them on approaching Henencourt was the blessed Sergeant Fry and his divine cookers full of steaming rum and cocoa, nectar and ambrosia in one, a drink for heroic men. Corporal Allen here arrested a man as a spy. He turned out to be a press*

photographer of the Illustrated London News, *and kindly sent copies of his snaps to Captain Llewellyn's home.'*

When the battalion was reunited at Senlis it was ascertained that three officers and 38 men had been killed, with a further 38 being missing. There were 174 wounded. The Dorsets took held the line from Aveluy Wood to Albert over Easter. The retreat was over and Captain A. H. Mitchell, among those awarded a Military Cross, paid a tribute to his men:

> *'It is all the more creditable, to those who took part in the battle that they rose above the adversities by which they were daily surrounded, and to a man upheld the fine traditions of the regiment.'*

While it was resting at Pernois, during April, the battalion received reinforcements of 23 officers and 735 other ranks. They enjoyed particularly successful brigade horse and transport shows on 23 May, with the Dorsets winning prizes for the best six teams and limbers, plus the best six pack mules – 'they came from Wareham, the faithful brutes' – which carried machine-gun ammunition and parts. There was also a first and a third in prizes for the best single mule. Battalion sports day followed on the 25th. The commanding officer, Major A. K. D. Hall, handed over to Major E. S. Weldon.

Back in the line, near Beaumont Hamel on 8 June 1918, the battalion carried out a daring raid along Y-Ravine. The element of surprise was maintained and the fighting was at close-quarters. Sixteen officers and 500 men rushed the enemy positions with bayonets, grenades and machine-guns. The regimental history, having detailed numerous individual actions, concludes:

> *'It was a fierce and murderous work of not an hour's duration – one of the three definite occasions when blood was hot for killing, and the Dorsets showed their fangs in real anger and slew their enemies face to face.'*

Lieutenant E. J. Leat and L. W. Forde were killed, along with nine other ranks. Sergeant Gerrard from Evershot who was one of the 'originals'. There were 29 missing and 117 wounded. Captain Davies, the Medical Officer, emerged from the aid post 'covered in blood from head to foot'. An estimated 150 Germans had been killed and several prisoners taken.

The surviving officers had coffee and rum with their eggs and bacon in the morning, with the Brigadier at Acheux, and the battalions – the East Yorks had also taken part – paraded in the afternoon. The Army Commander, General Sir Julian Byng, sent his congratulations. It was a morale-boosting success.

Captain Green and Major Shaw were the only officers remaining from the Wareham days when a battalion dinner was held on 13 July 1918 to celebrate the third anniversary of their arrival in France. Yorkshire-born Captain Green 'had a humorous but vulgar bulldog, whose tenacity was shared by his master'. An earlier battalion dog was the French poodle which accompanied Captain the Honourable Evelyn Hewitt DSO, a Boer War veteran, in the spring of 1917.

6TH BATTALION, DORSETSHIRE REGIMENT

The battalion moved forward to Corbie after the German line collapsed on 8 August 1918. They were at St Pierre Divion on when orders came that the Dorsets – led by A-Company under Major Shaw – were to lead the advance into the ruins of Thiepval. Major Shaw won the DSO for the 'soaked and sleepless' crossing of the River Ancre at Logging Lane on the 23rd. B-Company, under Lieutenant F. W. Woods, captured Common Trench but Lieutenant J. A. Maben was killed on the exposed flank.

At 01.00 on the 24th, Company Sergeant Major E. England was killed on the approach to Stuff Redoubt – which also features in the 5th Battalion's story – and Lieutenant-Colonel Weldon slipped on to 'the sharp end of a screw picket'. The advance had to be checked in the dark but daylight showed that the enemy had fled, leaving their dead and abandoning their stores. Three platoons of D-Company, under Lieutenant Searle, who had been posted missing, 'were found happily sitting on the furthest objective of the previous night'. The advance passed Monquet Farm, where the 5th Dorsets had fought in 1916, as the division proceeded to double objectives at Pozieres and Courcelette. The 6th Battalion 'spearhead' had advanced three miles, capturing 50 machine-guns and taking 350 German prisoners.

On 26 August, after the officers' horses had been brought forward for the first time, the Dorsets were given the central sector for an attack on Flers, to start at 01.00 next day. The plan was changed and started at 03.30, with an effective dash, but was blunted at 07.00 as a fresh German division counter-attacked. Lieutenant F. W. Woods, Second-Lieutenant G. Houghton, and 40 men were killed. An officer and ten men had been killed earlier in the action. There were 25 missing and 172 men wounded.

Lieutenant Davies, the medical officer, was also injured and his place taken by Lieutenant Leinis of the United States Army – who was killed the following day when the aid post was hit by a shell. During the funerals later in the week, Major Welman's horse – Snowball from Wareham – received his second shrapnel wound.

The attack resumed on 1 September, at Le Transloy, without much success, though the battalion diary notes that Captain Murray, helped by his servant, 'captured a party of 49 men and an officer'. They day ended with a gale and torrential rain. On the 11th the whole of the 17th Division was taken out of the line, after 22 days of action, during which it had advanced 19 miles. In the wider picture, 34,250 German prisoners had been taken in the first phase of the Battle of Bapaume, along with 270 artillery pieces.

Back in action again, on 18 September, Lieutenant T. H. Timberlake, with C-Company, captured Vaucelette Farm (and received the MC). Major Shaw unexpectedly captured three Germans when he found them sheltering in an old British dug-out beside the railway embankment:

> *'They meant no harm and were glad to be out of it.'*

The division as a whole captured 19 officers and 1,050 men but encountered stiff resistance from nearby Gouzeaucourt. The battalion confused its geography and ended up securing Quentin Redoubt by mistake. Lieutenant C. Morris turned the German machine-guns on the enemy (for an MC). Lieutenant L. P. Brooker came out of the smoke and recognised the place, as he had been there in March, and then they found an old British notice-board as 'proof positive'.

On 19 September, Lieutenants C. R. Kent and H. T. Parrish held Lancashire Trench. Battalion headquarters remained in Gauche Wood, with some degree of home comforts as the German cavalry had left behind their stock of red wine and their equivalent of 'Tommy Cookers'. Between Flers and Gauche Wood – in the second phase of the 'Great Advance' – the battalion had lost 22 men killed, 3 missing and 168 wounded. It was on 29 September that Hindenburg asked President Wilson for an armistice.

On 10 October, after passing the Hindenburg Line, the Dorsets were welcomed with jugs of coffee at the doorsteps as they advanced through Audencourt. Here the 1st Battalion, Dorsetshire Regiment, had fought over the same ground in August 1914. Similar welcomes awaited at Beaumont and Inchy. Having announced themselves as 'L'Armee Britannique,' the men were feted as liberators. Brigadier Shaw declined the offer of silk sheets from the lady of the house he had chosen for his headquarters. The women said they had wanted to kiss him, but found him 'too serious', and therefore embraced his groom.

On 10 October they were facing opposition from Neuvilly, firmly defended above a ravine on the River Selle. Machine-gunners, holding the houses, held back the Dorsets. Second-Lieutenant Parrish won an MC for retrieving a wounded man, but had been injured himself. He died from the wounds at the end of the war.

On 11 October, Sergeant Cole improvised a bridge out of a section of tramway which Private Davis manoeuvred into position. Captain H. W. Goodson MC started to lead C-Company across but was killed when a machine-gun opened up at point-bank range. The attempt continued but the bridge was not quite long enough and Sergeant Cole, with his Lewis guns, gave covering fire as the men withdrew. He won the Military Medal. Lieutenant Kent, sent down river from headquarters to find out what was happening, saved a wounded officer – at great danger – and gained the Military Cross. The padre, Captain I. Davies, up front with B-Company, was injured whilst tending the wounded. So too was the medical officer, American Lieutenant Lloyd-Wurster, who was awarded an MC. His staff were killed, as shells fell on the aid post, and stretcher-bearing parties were then led by Private Page, who gained the Military Medal.

The river was crossed the following day when the Royal Engineers prepared 30-feet footbridges and a bridge for two tanks (both of which crossed but one then stopped with engine trouble and the other when its caterpillar was hit). The Dorsets were relieved to be replaced and marched back to Montigny. Captain Goodson's body was brought to Audencourt for burial and the other Dorset dead were collected and buried by the river on the evening of the 18th.

The Germans mounted a last-ditch defence of the railway line in the early hours of 20 October. In the dark, under heavy fire, B-Company, under Captain C. F. Harrison (who gained the MC) approached machine-gunners and bombers who 'held out to the last'. Private Lamerton (given the MM) 'twice led on ahead and killed eight enemy unaided'. Lance-Corporal Boswell (also for an MM) personally took-out a machine-gun position on the embankment and killed its team. Lane-Corporal Dudley (ditto) cleared more machine-gun posts. Lieutenant W. A. Curtis (for the MC), coming round the flank with a C-Company platoon, personally eliminated 12 Germans. Second-Lieutenant Kent also charged headlong into a machine-gun post but was killed. Despite his wounds, Private Jordan (for the MM) maintained covering fire, with a Lewis gun. Sergeant Cole (another MM) found himself taking over as Company Sergeant Major and organised a four-man party to defend the attackers' rear. He succeeded in the objective of linking with the flanking battalion. Private Wright (for the MM) took on the hazardous task of acting as chief runner between battalion headquarters and the advancing platoons. Lieutenant Silk moved the advanced headquarters to the railway line at 04.00.

In daylight, Lieutenant-Colonel Shaw moved his own headquarters to the last house on the north side of Neuvilly. He found German mail, brown bread, butter and eggs. Captain Knapp discovered a bottle of brandy and the regimental history is loathe to spoil the anecdote:

> *'Undoubtedly there was a piano.'*

The *History of the Dorsetshire Regiment, 1914-1919*, tells us that other battalions brought in hundreds of prisoners, but the Dorsets only nine.

> *'There might have been two less. An 18-year-old runner, sent to deliver a message to rear headquarters by the river, escorted a stretcher carried by two prisoners. After handing over* [the casualty] *to the Medical Officer, he asked – "Shall I do them in now, Sir?" He was wounded by shrapnel in the face, but remained at duty.'*

The account indicates that on this occasion there was little desire or opportunity for taking prisoners:

> *'The estimated German dead in the battalion area was 200, mostly bayoneted.'*

So ended the Battle of the Salle. After they moved back to Inchy, Lieutenant-Colonel Shaw described it as the hardest battle of the advance. A platoon commander at Worgret, who was to suffer for the rest of his life from wounds received in 1915, Colonel Shaw then left on home leave. Lieutenant-Colonel Weldon resumed command. Morris Harvey and his 'Scroungers' – the brigade concert party – entertained the man in a barn at Neuvilly.

The next objective was Locquignol in the Mormal Forest where fighting through the oak and beech trees became a novel form of warfare. Reaching the village, on 5 November, cost the battalion 12 killed, 1 missing and 75 wounded. It was their last fighting of the war, which ended at Eclaibes, when 'three cheers were given for the King' on news of the Armistice, and they marched back to Berlaimont.

Forty-one miners were first to be demobilised. Neuvilly and its tough fight were remembered on 4 December 1918 when King George V visited the battleground with the Prince of Wales and Prince Albert (Duke of York). The visit was conducted by Major-General Robertson who brought the royal party 'informally through the cheering division'. There was much wine at Christmas followed by 'gradual dissolution':

> *'By February 28th the honourable discharge of horses and mules began.'*

The remaining men were deloused at Le Havre on 19 May and disembarked in Southampton on the 24th. They were left to disband themselves, Captain J. Bessell records, with his last entry in the battalion diary:

> *'No orders received since landing in England.'*

The battalion's death toll, including one casualty before it left England, was 44 officers and 757 other ranks.

fifteen

The Bournemouth Contribution

THOUGH IT WAS PART of Hampshire until 1974, the Victorian new town of Bournemouth sprawled beside and across Dorset's eastern boundary, and formed the region's main conurbation. Bournemouth's great send-off for the troops was a drumhead service in Meyrick Park on 4 October 1914. Key personnel gad already been mobilised after 'the lights went out all over Europe' – to quote the Foreign Secretary, Sir Edward Grey – following the assassination by Serbians of Archduke Franz Ferdinand of Austria in Sarajevo, on 29 June 1914. The British Expeditionary Force, dismissed by Kaiser Wilhelm II as 'a contemptible little army', was mobilised and sailed for France and Belgium within weeks of the declaration of war on 4 August 1914.

Drumhead service in Meyrick Park, Bournemouth, on 4 October 1914.

From the church of St John the Evangelist in Boscombe, Revd E. J. Kennedy found himself at Bustard Camp on Salisbury Plain. There he was awoken by the delivery of a telegram at 05.00 hours on 17 September 1914:

> *'You have been selected for immediate foreign service. Report yourself early to-morrow morning at the War Office.'*

He was appointed Chaplain Major to the British Expeditionary Force in Belgium and attached to the 7th Division under Lieutenant-General Sir Henry Rawlinson. Major Kennedy recorded that All Fools' Day in 1915 was marked by a pilot from the Royal

Flying Corps crossing the German lines and dropping 'a new kind of bomb' which bounced across the trenches. He had delivered a football, on which was written:

'The first of April, you blighters.'

He also told the story of the man who was hit in the wrist by a bullet. 'Got it,' he shouted. Then he produced a mouth-organ and played 'Home, Sweet, Home'. Kennedy mused:

'Who but an English Tommy could, or would, do that? No wonder that the French are puzzled by this strange composition of humanity with which they are fighting as allies.'

Revd E. J. Kennedy, from Bournemouth, as Chaplain Major to the British Expeditionary Force.

On the other hand the Tommy may have been showing delight and relief on receiving his return ticket to Blighty. While returning to England in the hospital ship *Carisbrooke Castle*, the sick Major Kennedy found himself in the next bed to a German officer who observed, Napoleon-style, that 'the contemptible little army' never knew when it was beaten. Neither did the vicar from Boscombe. He cut shot his recuperation to embark on a lecture tour, to Birkenhead and Liverpool, and again fell ill. After coming back home he died, within the week, on 25 October 1915. Though he had such a short war, he captured imagery 'both grave and gay' including the bird-song that punctuated 18-pounder artillery barrages 'as peacefully and merrily as in quiet English fields'.

Henry Page Croft (1881-1947), the town's member of Parliament – who had represented what was still known as the Christchurch constituency since 1910 – went off to war with the 1st Battalion, Hertfordshire Regiment. Mentioned in despatches and promoted Brigadier-General in February 1916 he was returned after the Great War, in 1918, for the new Bournemouth seat and remained in place until 1940 when he was created Baron Croft of Bournemouth. He then sat in the House of Lords as Under-Secretary of State for War. Lord Croft's life autobiography, *My Life of Strife*, was published posthumously in 1949.

Second-Lieutenant Gwilym Jones, only son of the minister of Richmond Hill Congregational Church, won the Military Cross. He was gassed while leading a platoon of the 2nd Battalion, Cheshire Regiment, on the Western Front. Though he returned to action he was wounded again and transferred to the Royal Flying Corps where he became a ferry pilot, delivering aeroplanes from England to war zones for the remainder of the conflict. Gwilym Jones then worked in the Leverhulme plantations of the Gold Coast, West Africa, and was an honorary district commissioner. He died there of blood poisoning after skidding and falling from his motorcycle in 1923.

Two young Bournemouth men were posthumously awarded the Victoria Cross for valour. Corporal Cecil Noble, late of St Clement's School, died while serving with the Rifle Brigade at Neuve Chappelle in March 1915. Sergeant Frederick Riggs survived action in Gallipoli and on the Somme, where he won the Military Medal, but fell with the Yorks and Lancaster Regiment while leading his platoon against a German machine-gun strong-point in 1918. He had attended Malmesbury Park School.

THE BOURNEMOUTH CONTRIBUTION

Sixty men from St Michael's parish failed to return from the Great War. St John's church at Moordown also lost many of its young men. Servers Reginald Burt, George Ivamy, Cecil Frank Ivamy and Harold Frederick Thompson were killed in action, as was chorister and typesetter Charles Henry Austin. Then, when it was over, the influenza pandemic took its toll. Gunner Arthur Harris died when he came home on leave in November 1918.

John Burden and William Laidlaw returned not only with their health but the Military Medal. Another local hero was Dr William Henry Putsey. When he died in 1922, he was said to have been the last surviving officer of HMS *Condor*, in which Admiral Lord Charles Beresford bombarded Alexandria.

Bournemouth and Christchurch were to have a lasting role in the evolution of military bridging, climaxing in the Sir Donald Coleman Bailey and his Bailey Bridges of the Second World War, which began when 502 (Wessex) Field Company of the Royal Engineers moved from Taunton to Iford Camp on 18 October 1915. Their first experience of pontooning was to try and tackle the fiercely tidal Avon Run between Mudeford and Hengistbury Head. In the *Narrative* of their story, Major C. L. Fox recorded how Lance-Corporal Jones and his crew:

This little card I send to you.
With greetings kind & wishes true
And if you read between the lines
Lots of kisses too you'll find !

Card from home to Sapper Frank Foxall in France.

'... flung themselves likes shipwrecked mariners on to the further shore, and just saved a disaster, amid the shouts and laughter of their comrades.'

As well as the 'toil of bridge-building' they were also required to march eight miles daily and to practice 'knots and lashings' tied 'behind our backs or with eyes shut'. They then moved into Waterloo-period buildings in Barrack Road and carried out 'squad-drill' and 'company drill' in nearby Christchurch recreation ground and on the Barracks field. In December the sappers' next short move was back across the River Stour – which they had been bridging – through the streets of Pokesdown to a camp at Southbourne. There was some confusion after 9 December 1915, when they were drafted to the 57th Division as part of the 'Central Force' to defend Great Britain, and left for Whitstable, Kent. They found stores being sent – often in duplicate – to three separate addresses in and around Bournemouth and four across Kent. The company found itself at Imber, on Salisbury Plain, before the inevitable departure to France, on the *Archangel* to Le Havre, in February 1917.

sixteen

Dorset's War Poets

SUB-LIEUTENANT RUPERT BROOKE (1887-1915) fully qualifies as a Dorset war poet. He was introduced to the county when he holidayed at his grandfather's home in Bournemouth but soon despaired of the resort's 'decrepit invalids' and went off to rent rooms in Lulworth Cove which he described as the 'most beautiful village in England'. The famous words about dying for his country were penned in Blandford Camp, in C-Lines on the east side beside Blackland Plantation, as he trained with the Anson Battalion of the Royal Naval Division in 1914:

Rupert Brooke left for war from Blandford.

> *'I spend Christmas in looking after drunken stokers. One of them has been drunk since 7 am; he neither eats nor drinks, but dances a complicated step up and down his hut, singing "How happy I am, how happy I am" – a short, fat inelegant man, in stockinged feet. What wonders we are! There's no news – occasional scares. On Wednesday I (don't tell a soul) started a sonnet. What a fall!'*

One of his five sonnets from 1914 – 'The Soldier' – was to prove prophetic:

> *'If I should die, think only this of me:*
> *That there's some corner of a foreign field*
> *That is for ever England. There shall be*
> *In that rich earth a richer dust concealed;*
> *A dust when England bore, shaped, made aware,*
> *Gave, once, her flowers to love, her ways to roam,*
> *A body of England's breathing English air,*
> *Washed by rivers, blest by suns of home.*
>
> *And think, this heart, all evil shed away,*
> *A pulse in the eternal mind, no less*
> *Gives somewhere back the thoughts by England given;*
> *Her sights and sounds; dreams happy as her day;*
> *And laughter, learnt of friends; and gentlemen,*
> *In hearts at peace, under an English heaven.'*

Rupert Brooke wrote from Canford Manor, the home of Lord and Lady Wimborne, on 24 January 1915:

> *'These proofs have come. My muse, panting all autumn under halberd and cuirass, could but falter these syllables through her vizor. God, they're in the rough, these five camp-children – [numbers] 4 and 5 are good enough, and there are phrases in the rest.'*

To write, properly, in wartime required longer periods of serenity, he remarked. Though Brooke arrived in the Middle East, en route to Gallipoli, he never fought the Turks. Having contracted blood poisoning from a mosquito bite, in the days before antibiotics, he became comatose from fever and died on the troopship *Franconia* on Friday 23 April 1916. His friend Denis Browne took charge of the funeral on the Aegean island of Skyros:

> *'We buried him the same evening in an olive-grove where he had sat with us on Tuesday – one of the loveliest places on earth, with grey-green olives round him, one weeping above his head; the ground covered with flowering sage, bluish-grey, and smelling more delicious than any flower I know. The path up to it from the sea is narrow and difficult and very stony; it runs by the bed of a dried-up torrent. We had to post men with lamps every twenty yards to guide the bearers. He was carried from the boat by his A-Company petty officers, led by Platoon-Sergeant Saunders; and it was with enormous difficulty that they got the coffin up the narrow way. The journey of a mile took two hours.'*

Brooke's manuscript of 'The Soldier'.

Another poet, killed at Gallipoli on 4 June 1915, was signals officer Captain Ainslie Douglas Talbot, whose love letters to Mrs Dorothy 'Dorfie' Slingsby, donated to the Imperial War Museum, were researched by Michael Moyniham for his book *Greater Love* in 1980. He quoted from one entitled 'Studland Bay':

> *'Sweet Bay of Studland, patron of my lay,*
> *May thy propitious muse my song promote;*
> *Close to thy waters, she and I did stray,*
> *and there converse on worlds so far remote.'*

Dorothy was overwhelmed by news of his death and joined the Queen Alexandra's Imperial Military Nursing Service in order to obtain a posting to the Middle East theatre. She served in Egypt and is thought to have landed at Cape Helles in November 1915 but was turned back before she could reach Captain Talbot's grave. Dorothy's last wish, in 1975, was for her ashes to be scattered on W-Beach at Gallipoli.

DORSET IN THE FIRST WORLD WAR

Bournemouth provided the last holiday home in 1914 for the remarkably talented Isaac Rosenberg (1890-1918) from Stepney whose career as a private soldier also terminated in long-lasting fame as a war poet. He stayed with the Cohen family at 195 Wimborne Road which, before re-numbering, was on the south side of Peters Hill in Winton.

Thomas Hardy (1840-1928) was at the height of his celebrity as an international novelist and poet. Though never a soldier himself, he had immersed himself, retrospectively, in the military causes and customs of past generations. This conflict, however, brought demands for an instant commentary. As a 74-year-old on the Home Front at Max Gate, Dorchester, he wrote a sonnet entitled 'On the Belgian Expatriation' for Sir Hall Caine's fund-raising *King Albert's Book*, sponsored by The *Daily Telegraph*, in October 1914:

> *'I dreamt that people from the Land of Chimes*
> *Arrived one autumn morning with their bells,*
> *To hoist them on the towers and citadels*
> *Of my own country, that the musical rhymes*
>
> *Rung by them into space and measured times*
> *Amid the market's daily stir and stress,*
> *And the night's empty starlit silentness,*
> *Might solace souls of this and kindred climes.*
>
> *Then I awoke; and lo, before me stood*
> *The visioned ones, but pale and full of fear;*
> *From Bruges they came, and Antwerp, and Ostend,*
>
> *No carillons in their train. Vicissitude*
> *Had left these tinkling to the invaders ear,*
> *And ravaged street, and smouldering gable-end.'*

Further poems inspired by the plight of the Belgians included 'An Appeal to America on Behalf of the Belgian Destitute' and 'Cry of the Homeless'. The more general theme of war and patriotism was addressed by 'Men Who March Away' (published in *The Times* as 'Song of the Soldiers'), 'His Country' and 'England to Germany in 1914'. In 1915 the titles were 'The Pity of It', 'In Time of Wars and Tumults', 'In Time of 'The Breaking of Nations', 'Then and Now , 'Often When Warring', 'The Dead and the Living One', 'Before Marching and After' and 'A New Year's Eve in War Time'. The penultimate was dedicated to 'F.W.G.' – the virtual adopted son of Florence and Thomas Hardy – Second-Lieutenant Frank William George of the 5th Battalion, the Dorsetshire Regiment, who fell in a Turkish bayonet attack in the Valley of Death on the Gallipoli peninsula on 21 August 1915. 'Then and Now', published in *The Times*, compared modern 'total war' with King Herod's biblical slaughter of children.

Do not imagine that Hardy was a pacifist. Having deplored the truce in No Man's Land, he regarded conscription as inevitable – producing 'A Call to National Service' in March 1917 – and urged the 'crushing utterly' of rebellious Sinn Feiners in Dublin.

Dorchester sage Thomas Hardy.

Then on 9 November 1916, Thomas and Florence were invited by the Commandant of the Prisoner of War Camp at Poundbury, Dorchester, to meet the Germans. It transformed Hardy's attitude, Mrs Hardy told their friend Sir Sydney Cockerell:

> *'T.H.'s heart kind heart melted at the sight of the wounded and he expressed his sympathy with them by eloquent gestures to which they responded in a most friendly manner … and now he is sending them some of his books in German, for their library.'*

He remained notably less productive as the war dragged through its endless stalemate and became reflective with 'I Met a Man', 'I Looked Up from My Writing' and 'The Coming of the End'. By then, as with 'Afterwards', there was no longer any mention of the war.

'Jezreel', published in *The Times* on 27 September 1918, recorded the capture from the

Turks of an ancient city in Palestine (now Zerin, Israel) by General Edmund Allenby's Egyptian Expeditionary Force. Did they realise, Hardy wondered, that this was the setting of a biblical slaughter, involving King Ahab and Queen Jezebel, between deities Baal and Jehovah? Finally, for the Armistice Day supplement in *The Times* on 11 November 1920, Hardy chose a phrase from two of the gospels and wrote 'And There Was a Great Calm'. Why the war, Hardy asks? He expresses particular grief for the suffering horses and other animals:

> *'Calm fell. From Heaven distilled a clemency;*
> *There was peace on earth, and silence in the sky;*
> *Some could, some could not, shake off the misery:*
> *The Sinister Spirit sneered: "It had to be!"*
> *And again the Spirit of Pity whispered, "Why?"'*

seventeen

Returnees Bring New Dorset Dialect

THE PRESENCE AT BLANDFORD CAMP of the Royal Naval Division and the repatriation of the wounded to Red Cross hospitals brought a new language to the county. It was rapidly imitated by the young. The Army expressions of previous days had been largely corruptions of Arabic and Hindustani words but speech patterns of the current war were a mix of cosmopolitan and cockney with lashings of rhyming slang. The failure of a waitress to cope with the varying demands of a group of convalescents was met with the riposte:

'Guess she's been taking a sleigh-ride!'

Cocaine was known as 'snow' and the 'sleigh-ride' implied she was drugged. Speech in the wider community was also coming under the influence of the war. Many times a day there were tasks to be undertaken 'to do our bit' and people were always being exhorted to 'carry on'. Whenever there was anything that could be conceivably imagined as a target it was to be 'strafed' (flies were no longer swotted). 'Not 'arf' hardly sounded out of place, however, as southern English youth had never bothered to use their aitches before they left for the war.

Rhyming slang sounded the most awful. To appear in the street with a red nose was to invited the comment 'a cold I suppose' ('I suppose' meant nose). For eye it was 'mince pie' and arm became 'false alarm'. 'Cherry ripe' was pipe and 'plates of meat' were feet. At that level there was also 'Sieda' (the Indian and Egyptian veterans' word for socks). To confuse things further, the Australians restored its genuine meaning – 'Good morning'. Eye was 'mince pie'. Socks were 'almond rocks'. And just about anything was more acceptable than 'daisy roots' for boots.

'I like your Chevy Chase' was a compliment upon one's facial appearance. Less romantically, despite the hostilities, the pre-war 'German band' lived on for hand. Far-fetched tales were 'only a buzz'. When anyone had luck or fortune of any kind it was 'jam' or 'jammy'. Being absent was 'chucking a dummy'. The married quarters at the camp was known as 'the Home Farm'. Dora was the Defence of the Realm Act, 1916, which did so much to curtail and restrict normal life. An 'ATA wallah' was a teetotaller (the initials being those of the Army Temperance Association). 'Government dough' was wholemeal flour, with people complaining they could not digest the healthy and husky full-fibre content. Worse were the catch phrases, all being endlessly repeated:

'What ho, she bumps ... Give it the bird ... Now we shan't be long ... Swinging the lead ... I don't think.'

This all sounds a world away from one of Dorset's most evocative memorials of the Great War. The 'News Office' at Iwerne Minster was originally erected as a canopy over the parish pump at the junction in the centre of the village. Here, among the thatched cottages of banded flint and brick, notice boards were erected beside recruitment posters. These extolled the men of Iwerne – pronounced 'You-Urn' – to volunteer to 'Fight for King and Country' as hostilities spread across the globe. Panels were filled with postcards, photographs and snippets of news that attracted growing attention as the news from the Western Front took on a sharper edge.

Clippings from national newspapers included accounts of the world's first air-raid, by a Zeppelin airship over Great Yarmouth, on the evening of 19 January 1915. Soon there was no more available room and a purpose-built stone shelter – the name of which graduated from 'News Office' to 'War Office' – was provided nearby. Open fronted, beneath a lamp and a winged angel, it was soon lined with displays. Countrymen thronged around it in a state of fearful anticipation, as details of the unfolding carnage emerged despite the constraints of natural reserve and official censorship. In some cases these poignant letters were from soldiers and sailors whose names were already in other postbags carrying casualty lists from the next series of engagements.

From December 1917, in return for this stream of information sent to him by combatants, estate owner James Harmsworth Ismay (1867-1930) of Iwerne Minster House began publication of the three-weekly *Iwerne Times* for those serving overseas. Pastoral news from the sheep-leazes of Cranborne Chase and the dairies of the Blackmore Vale included details of hurdle production in the coppices and the latest hogsale prices. *Buy War Savings Certificates* was the title of the latest movie film to be shown in the village. The sting came at the beginning of the newspaper, with the warning that this comforting news from home would be accompanied by the dose of reality that everyone dreaded. Second-Lieutenant Ismay of the Hampshire Carabiniers Yeomanry (who transferred to the Dorsetshire Yeomanry) warned his readers:

'I'm afraid my first news to you must be sad, for it will tell you of the deaths of your friends.'

Ismay had sold the White Star Fleet to American financier J. Pierpont Morgan in 1902. This provided the cash for buying 1880-built Iwerne Minster House from Lord Wolverton. Ismay, Imrie and Company continued to manage the Ocean Steam Navigation Company – universally known as the White Star Line – and James's elder brother, Joseph Bruce Ismay (1862-1937) chose the name for their thirteenth great liner. She was the 46,328-ton *Titanic*. Bruce Ismay was among the 711 survivors from the total of 2,201 who sailed on her maiden voyage in 1912.

In the Great War the sister-vessels were troopships or floating hospitals. At home in Dorset the Ismay brothers pursued their traditional countryside recreations of shooting, hunting and fishing. The other guns were seldom out of mind. I used to be told by old people in Bournemouth that they clearly heard the barrage that opened the offensive on the first day of the Battle of the Somme, on 1 July 1916.

eighteen

Float-planes, Portland and the War at Sea

THE POTENTIAL FOR NAVAL aviation had been established on 28 July 1914 when Royal Navy pilot Arthur Longmore launched a 14-inch torpedo from a Short seaplane. On 9 May 1916, at Kingsnorth, Kent, a 500-pound bomb was dropped from 4,000 feet from a Short 184 seaplane. Dropped with the aid of a Bourdillon &Tizard bomb-sight, it successfully hit the armour-clad roof that was the target.

Royal Navy seaplanes were based at Portland.

Portland Royal Naval Air Station was established in The Mere marshes between the Chesil Beach and Portland Harbour on 26 September 1916. It was initially designated as shore-base HMS *Sereptia*. The expansion that followed included a seaplane shed while the lagoon beside the bunkering oil tanks became the home-base for 12 Short & Wright float-planes of No. 416 and 417 Flights, which amalgamated to form 241 Naval Air Squadron in 1918.

Four 9.2-inch guns were installed in Blacknor Fort, in Victorian emplacements midway along Portland's western cliffs, in a commanding position overlooking Lyme Bay.

The sea continued to be the traditional enemy. The Navy's armed trawler HMT *King Heron* was driven on to the ledges off Old Harry Rocks, Studland, on 13 November 1915. Poole's lifeboat, *Harmar*, had to make two attempts to reach the vessel in a heavy sea and surging tide. Another armed trawler towed her upwind so that the lifeboat could lift off the ten sailors, and then reattached the line to tow the *Harmar* back to Poole.

On the evening of 3 August 1916, a German submarine surfaced beside the schooner *Fortuna*, 15 miles south-south-west of Portland Bill. The Falmouth vessel was carrying scrap iron from Le Havre to Swansea. The U-boat's deck-gun was trained on the *Fortuna* as German officers placed charges on board. She was blown-up half an hour later. Her crew, who had been put in a boat, were later rescued by the *Joanna*, also in sail, and landed at Plymouth. The same submarine was also seen intercepting and sinking the sailing barge *Ivo*.

The following morning, 24 miles south-south-west of Portland Bill, it was the turn of the Bridgwater schooner *Erme-nilda* which was carrying 155 tons of granite from Guernsey to Poole. Her four crewmen were picked up by a Russian steamship.

The 1,342-ton West Hartlepool collier *Spiral* was also stopped on 4 August 1916 by a German submarine, identified as *UB-18*. The location was 14 miles south-east of Portland Bill. In transit from the Tyne to Bordeaux, she carried a cargo of coal, which was a major strategic import to war-torn France, at the rate of 1,500,000 tons a month for the duration of the conflict.

Floating seaplane dock in Portland Harbour.

On 22 October 1916, the Royal Navy drifter HMT *Fame* was blown on to the Hook Sands, off the entrance to Poole Harbour, by a south-easterly wind. Seven sailors were taken off by the Poole lifeboat, *Harmar*, as the stricken boat rolled over and began to break up.

The Norwegian freighter *Daphne*, 1,388 tons, was torpedoed and sunk on 11 November 1916 by *UB-16* while steaming up-Channel off Portland, from Newport to Rouen. She was carrying coal, as was the 3,806-ton Bergen steamship *Finn*, torpedoed by *UB-26*, 40 miles south-west of Portland Bill on 19 November 1916. The ship was en route from the Tyne to Genoa.

Fishing boats, working 25 miles south-west of Portland Bill, were targeted by a German submarine on 28 November 1916. Crews were taken off the wooded smacks *Amphotrite* and *Provident*, which were then sunk by gunfire and scuttling charges.

Heavily armed but disguised naval vessels, designed to look just like the merchant ships from which they had been converted, were a bright idea adopted by Winston Churchill, First Lord of the Admiralty. Their deadly combination of theatrics and trickery paid dividends as these Q-ships accounted for a total of 12 U-boats. One of these successful actions took place 24 miles south-west of Portland Bill on 30 November 1916.

The day began inauspiciously for German minelaying submarine *UB-19*. She surfaced beside the German-owned schooner *Behrend*, now flying the red ensign as the vessel had been confiscated by the Admiralty, while berthed at Arbroath on the day that war began. The sailing ship was en route from London to Brest with a cargo of guano fertiliser. Her sinking was followed by the arrival of a more tempting target.

The submarine surfaced at the side of the Q-ship *Penhurst*. Action stations! Screens were thrown aside and the white ensign went up the halyard as the first of 83 shells pounded into the doomed U-boat. Of the Germans who jumped into the sea, 16 survived to be taken prisoner.

Steaming up-Channel, eight miles south-east of Portland Bill at 22.30 hours on 8 December 1916, the 5,620-ton tanker *Conch* was torpedoed and sunk. She was on the last leg of a voyage from Rangoon for Burmah Oil, carrying 7,000 tons of benzene, to the Thames refineries. No warning had been given and the first anyone knew of the presence of *UB-23* was a thud, followed by a great tower of flame as burning oil engulfed the bridge and destroyed all but one of the lifeboats. Of the crew, a total of 28 were killed – many of them Chinese – although a similar number were able to escape, mostly by jumping into the sea. The forward tanks continued to burn through the night and the ship went down at 07.00 hours the following morning.

On 28 December 1916 the French barque *Union*, 563 tons, foundered off Portland Bill but was a victim of the weather rather than the submarines. War losses resumed on 20 January 1917 with the Danish schooner *Standard*, carrying china clay from Fowey to Leith, 13 miles south of Portland Bill. She was followed by the 2,548-ton West Hartlepool collier *Romsdalen*, torpedoed by *U-84* ten miles south-west of the Bill while carrying coke from Newport to Calais on 17 February 1917. The same submarine used the remainder of her torpedoes on the 2,233-ton Liverpool steamship *Valdes*, passing seven miles south of the Bill on 18 February. As she went down, 11 seamen were lost, in what was intended as a supply mission to support troops on the Western Front. They were carrying flour for bread and hay for the horses from Manchester to Cherbourg.

Geography played a part in the German submarine offensive during the second half of the war. Beachy Head, St Catherine's Point and Portland Bill joined Start Point and the Lizard as prime danger points where U-boats waited between shipping and the shore. The new generation of ocean-going enemy submarines were 240 feet in length and displaced 820 tons, carrying a 4.1-inch deck gun and 16 torpedoes. These were mainly deployed in the Western Approaches, but the Channel and North Sea were infested with smaller 100ft craft with double tubes and a total of four torpedoes, operating from Zeebrugge and Ostend. They could also lay mines.

'The position is exceedingly grave,' Admiral Sir John Jellicoe, as Chief of Naval Staff, warned the First Lord of the Admiralty and the War Cabinet in February 1917. He foresaw a situation in which it would be impossible to continue waging war if such losses continued. Admiral Sir David Beatty was persuaded to relinquish eight of his best destroyers, from the elite Grand Fleet, to sail south for the English Channel on anti-submarine patrols. Rear-Admiral Alexander Duff took command of a new Anti-Submarine Division. Other drastic measures had included the disguised Q-ships but the fear was that once their presence was known to U-boat captains, more shipping would be sunk on sight rather than being scuttled after the crews had been put in boats. The introduction of depth-charges and the convoy system did more than anything to reduce the losses.

The 3,073-ton freighter *Baygitano* was torpedoed by *UC-77*, inshore in Lyme Bay, on 18 March 1918, a mile-and-a-half south-west of Lyme Regis. Two of the crew were drowned but the remainder were safely taken off by the lifeboat from the Cobb, and other small craft which came to the aid of the sinking steamship. Built in 1903 and owned by the Bay Steam Ship Company, she was in ballast and returning from Le Havre to Cardiff, having delivered a cargo of coal. She is now known in Lyme as 'The Wreck'.

The *Moidart*, an 1878-built collier of 1,303 tons, was torpedoed and sunk seven miles south-east of Lyme Regis by *UC-77* on 9 June 1918. She was carrying a cargo of coal up-Channel from Barry, South Wales. Her crew of 15 were lost.

There was natural concern along the coast but the residents of Lyme Regis became something of a laughing stock for a spate of absurd U-boat alarms. One, which was actually reported to Scotland Yard, was that a German submarine base had been established below the Undercliff in Pinhay Bay. It arose from this story:

> '... *that a man was found unconscious on the rocks one day, who, when he came round, made the statement that while standing looking toward the land someone came up from behind and knocked him on the head.*'

Newly-built destroyers HMS Tyrian *and* Tetrarch *on speed trials off Anvil Point, Swanage.*

nineteen
Airfields and Airship Stations

GIVEN THE LIMITED RANGE of early aircraft, Dorset was far from the front line, but each county had to respond to the call from the Royal Flying Corps for ever more pilots. The war had started with just six squadrons, concentrated at Netheravon, Wiltshire, but Lord Kitchener increased this to 100 squadrons in 1916, and it doubled to 200 squadrons in 1917. By the end of the conflict there would be 10,800 combat casualties in the air.

Special flying schools, each with a training airfield, were established nationally in October 1917 to teach aerial fighting. There was already one in operation between Bournemouth and Poole at Talbot Village Aerodrome. It lay in the north-eastern extremity of the Borough of Poole across what is now the Talbot Campus of Bournemouth University. Among those young volunteers who came to grief was Second-Lieutenant Edward Rebbeck, from a mayoral estate-agency family in Bournemouth, who crashed nearby on 24 April 1916. His more fortunate Bournemouth-born namesake, who dropped his given first-name Leopold, was serving at the time in HMS *Erin*. He retired as Rear-Admiral Sir Edward Rebbeck (1901-83).

Organised flying, under the auspices of Bournemouth Aviation Company, moved to the new Ensbury Park Racecourse in 1917. This then lay in the Dorset parish of Kinson but is now entirely suburbanised, under Leybourne Avenue and adjoining streets in Northbourne, Bournemouth. Its toll of accidents included the death-crash of Major John Lockock on 22 July 1918.

There was, however, a priority need for Dorset aerial contributions to the real war. By 1917 the submarine menace in the English Channel was being countered by the Zero airship. This 112-feet SSZ type of Admiralty balloon was helium-filled and could remain airborne for ten hours. Though only armed with a Lewis gun, its presence could prove deadly to German U-boat commanders as the gunner doubled as a wireless operator. His prime role was to call and direct surface warships, from Portland,

Zero airship moored in pine trees at Upton Admiralty Air Station.

Portsmouth or Plymouth, to drop depth-charges. Such observation platforms effectively kept many enemy submarines underwater, at least in daylight, where they were no longer a threat. The main practical problem for their pilots was that such machines, being weightless, were difficult to manoeuvre.

To be tethered on the surface they each required a mooring pit, 30 feet wide and a similar depth, in order to accommodate the gondola and engine, so that wind resistance was minimised by bringing the supporting envelope down to ground level. Each coastal zone had its own airship station with pits, gas-holders, hangars, workshops and accommodation huts. There were three such establishments in Dorset.

The airship crash at Loders in 1918.

Upton Admiralty Air Station, hidden in heathland pines to the west of Poole, was a satellite station to that at Polegate, Sussex. Its strip of the coast was from St Alban's Head in the Isle of Purbeck to St Catherine's Point on the Isle of Wight.

The next stretch of western seaboard, to Portland Bill, was covered by Dorset's biggest and busiest air station. Moreton Admiralty Airship Station was established in 1918 on 355 acres of requisitioned land, at Higher Woodsford, stretching from the Wareham to Dorchester railway line to the hamlet beside Woodsford Castle. The site was entirely in the parish of Woodsford but for convenience was named for Moreton railway station, which lies a mile to the east, opposite the Frampton Arms.

The third Dorset establishment, operational from spring 1918 till the end of the war, was Toller Admiralty Airship Station. This operated as a satellite station to Mullion, Cornwall, and covered Lyme Bay from Portland Bill to Start Point. Naval back-up came from Plymouth as well as Portland. The site was established in wooded hills, a mile and a half west of the village of Toller Porcorum, to the north-west of Gray's Farm. Though taking its name from Toller the site was in Powerstock parish. A Zero airship crashed near the railway line at Loders while on an anti-submarine patrol from Mullion to Toller. Too much height had been lost over Bridport, after which the gondola clipped the tree-tops and then grounded on a grassy slope. The pilot, John Owner, and his crew stepped out unhurt.

Naval airship at Fort Grange, Portsmouth.

twenty
Heroes and Prisoners

DORSET MEN also served in all kinds of units all over the world. The Pope family from Wrackleford House, Stratton, made the biggest single contribution to the war effort. Alfred Pope (1842-1934), the Dorchester brewer, catalogued their efforts with stepson R. G. Bartlelot in *A Book of Remembrance: The Popes of Wrackleford* published in 1919 (with 'A Wessex Family during the Great War' being the alternative title on its spine). Alfred and Mrs Elizabeth Mary Pope had a total of 15 surviving children at the outbreak of the Great War. All eleven of the boys went to war, if one includes Sub-Lieutenant William Eldridge Pope (1881-1901), who lost his life from pneumonia on returning to Portsmouth in HMS *Hermione* from the Boxer Rebellion in China.

Eldest daughter Elizabeth Kate Pope worked with the Voluntary Aid Detachment of the Red Cross in Dorchester. Second daughter Violet Mary Pope married Lieutenant-Colonel Alan Haig-Brown DSO, the, youngest son of the headmaster at Charterhouse School, who served with the Middlesex Regiment. He was killed on 25 March 1918. Two 'die-hard' battalions, one commanded by Colonel Haig-Brown, the other by Colonel Otter:

Lieutenant-Colonel Alan Haig-Brown was killed at Achiet-le-Grand.

> '... put up a magnificent fight in the rear-guard action against an enemy attacking in numerical supreriotity of ten to one. For hours the two held on, the Middlesex with their flank exposed and the Queen's in similar predicament on the right, in a field near Achiet-le-Grand. Withdrawal was deferred till the enveloping movements of the enemy were nearly complete, and Alan, while directing the retirement of his men, was killed instantaneously by the fire of a machine-gun at close range.'

Third daughter Hilda Pope married Captain Herbert Henry Levy of the Army Service Corps. She spent the war with the Red Cross in Dorchester, Weymouth and Camberwell, and was then drafted to Calais. Fourth daughter Evelyn Grace Pope, who married Fordington vicar Revd Richard Grosvenor Bartelot, worked in the Red Cross bandaging depot in Dorchester.

Major Alfred Rolph Pope (1870-1951) ran the Territorial Forces Association office in Dorchester and marshalled the 4th Battalion, Dorsetshire Regiment, for active service.

Lieutenant-Colonel Edward Alexander Pope from Wrackleford.

Lieutenant-Colonel Edward Alexander Pope (1875-1919) of the Welsh Regiment, a veteran of the Boer War, lived at Woodbridge, Branksome Park. He was wounded in France in 1917 and suffered 'bronchial trouble, caused by mental strain and overwork'. He succumbed at the end of the war to 'disease contracted on active service'.

Sergeant George Clement Pope (born 1876) enlisted in the 1st Battalion, Dorsetshire Regiment, and survived to fish for trout again in the Frome at Wrackleford.

Captain Charles Alfred Whiting Pope (1877-1917) was put in charge of a detachment of the Royal Army Medical Corps and sent to Egypt on the troopship *Transylvania*. This was torpedoed in the Mediterranean, off Cape Vado, on 4 May 1917. Charles 'went down with the ship whilst dressing the wounds of the poor fellows who were hit by the explosion'.

Second-Lieutenant Percy Paris Pope (1882-1915) of the 1st Welsh Regiment was wounded and posted missing in a bayonet attack on Little Willie Trench beside Hohenzollern Redoubt during the Battle of Loos on 2 October 1915. For a while it was thought that he had been taken prisoner but nothing more was heard of him.

London lawyer Godfrey Pope (born 1885) left for Ceylon in 'the rubber boom' of 1910 and worked for another Dorset man, Mr Pitfield, on the Kahawattee and Serepama estates. In 1913 he bought a half share of the Arangalla Estate in Matala district. He had joined the Ceylon Planters' Rifle Corps and was refused leave to depart for the European war while a native uprising was a possibility.

Captain Albert Victor Pope (born 1887) joined the 14th (King's) Hussars in India and returned to England, to Bisley, as 'the best revolver shot in the Army' having scored 315 hits from 324 shots. In November 1915 he arrived in Basra with the India Expeditionary Force in Mesopotamia, making an impossible attempt at taking Baghdad from the Turks, which ended with a broken force falling back exhausted to Kut-el-Amara. Albert was with the force that eventually reached Baghdad, a year later, in March 1917. He went on to Ramadi and later led the advance party of a unit which continued across snow-covered mountains in Persia to the oil port of Baku on the Caspian Sea, in a secret raid against Turks and Bolsheviks in July 1918.

Lieutenant John Allen 'Jack' Pope (born 1888) joined brother Godfrey in Ceylon. He returned with a colonial contingent and enlisted in the King's Royal Rifle Corps. Having fought at Ypres and in the Battle of Guillemont, on the Somme, he 'was invalided home, suffering from shell-shock and gastritis'.

Major Decimus 'Decie' Pope (born 1889), won the Military Cross while fighting in France with a signals detachment of 8th Army Corps. He was one of the survivors of a group of officers blown up by a shell on 9 January 1917 near Boulogne. A colonel and a major died of their wounds and Decimus lay in hospital with a wound in his right thigh. He had been thrown through the air. Providentially, 'another splinter had gone through my pocket, smashed my pipe, and, after going through my tobacco pouch, landed in the centre of a thick notebook'.

Captain Cyril Pope (born 1891) went with the 1st Battalion, Bedfordshire Regiment, from facing resistance to Home Rule in Ulster, to the battles in Belgium with the British Expeditionary Force in August 1914. He was taken prisoner, in a wood in the dark, after going up to a group of German infiltrators, 'thinking them to be my own men'.

Similar stories can be told from across the county. Some came to national attention.

John Glossop, who retired to Bothenhampton as Vice-Admiral John Collings Taswell Glossop (1871-1934), commanded the cruiser HMAS *Sydney* when she sank the notorious German raider *Emden* in the Indian Ocean on 9 November 1914. Glossop, of Little Wych in Burton Road, was the brother of Mrs C. F. S. Sanctuary of Mangerton. He was a veteran of the Samoan troubles of 1899 – as a lieutenant in HMS *Royalist* – and reached the rank of captain in 1911. He might have emerged with more credit were it not for a swashbuckling party of 49 Germans under Kapitanleutnant Helmuth von Mucke who escaped and landed on British-owned Direction Island in the Cocos Keeling group off Western Australia.

They attacked its wireless telegraph station and proceeded to capture the schooner *Ayesha*. In this they made a rendezvous with a German freighter and took it across the Indian Ocean, successfully evading a British blockade of Arab dhows off Aden, to enter the Red Sea. They then took to the land, crossing Arabia by camel and suffering recurrent bouts of dysentery, typhus and malaria. They also endured three days of skirmishing with Bedouin tribesmen. Eventually the group reached El Ala and took the train through Turkish-occupied Damascus, to return to Europe after crossing half the world.

Finally, at Haidar Pasha, von Mucke proudly presented himself and fellow survivors, ready for duty, to a beaming Admiral Souchon and staff officers of the Mediterranean division of the Imperial German Navy:

> *'I report the landing squad from the* Emden*, five officers, seven petty officers, and thirty men strong.'*

For the British and the Australians, John Glossop remained the 'sink the *Emden*' hero, but the sequel took the gloss off the achievement and blocked the knighthood he thought he deserved. It was not until 1922 that he was promoted Rear-Admiral, and retired Vice-Admiral in 1927, with honours including Companion of the Bath, Officer of the Legion of Honour, and the Order of the Rising Sun (3rd class) from grateful allies in Japan.

Chief Petty Officer Ernest Pitcher (1888-1946), who was brought up in Swanage and attended the Board School there, came to fame in the middle of the Great War. He was severely wounded but stayed at his gun on 'a red hot deck' when the armed merchantman Q50 turned itself into HMS *Dunraven* as it was engaged by German submarine *UC-71* in the Bay of Biscay on 8 August 1917.

Huge clouds of steam were released from perforated pipes and ship used its unconcealed stern gun – deliberately ineffectually to lure the U-boat closer – between 10.58 hours and 12.25. Then the order was given to 'Abandon ship'. It was a ruse but black smoke from a German shell bellowed from the rear of the *Dunraven* as a fire threatened to explode her ammunition and depth charges. The Germans fired a torpedo at 13.20 after which a second draft of men abandoned ship in rafts. There were still 23 men hidden on board – manning two concealed guns and other armaments 'with shells exploding all around them' – though the Germans now regarded the ship as abandoned and crippled.

At 14.55 the submarine passed alongside the burning ship. The *Dunraven*'s captain fired two torpedoes. One missed but the other clanged against the submarine though it failed to explode. The three-hour engagement was over. The submarine headed for safety, and Germany, and the crippled *Dunraven* sank that evening as rescue ships arrived. Captain Gordon Campbell VC received a bar for his Victoria Cross and became the most decorated sailor of the Royal Navy during the Great War.

A Lieutenant and Petty Officer Pitcher also won the Victoria Cross, with the manner

Post-war raising of the Vindictive *blockship.*

The Vindictive *blockship which Victor Crutchley VC delivered to Ostend.*

of Pitcher's award being unusual in the way in which he was selected for the supreme honour, by the votes of his comrades. It was an action in which all had shown great courage. The VC, in effect, was awarded to the ship, and Pitcher was regarded by his mates as the most deserving recipient on behalf of them all. The *Dunraven* attack was described by Lieutenant-Commander Harold Acton VC as:

> *'... the greatest action of any Q-boat against a submarine. It was fought by a ship's company of heroes.'*

The gun crew's decoration was received by Pitcher from George V at Buckingham Palace on 5 December 1917. He was also awarded the French Medaille Militaire and the Croix de Guerre. Pitcher retired from the Royal Navy in 1927, becoming a woodwork teacher and the landlord of the Royal Oak at Herston, Swanage, before rejoining the Navy in 1939. Having served throughout the Second World War, at Poole, Portland and Yeovilton Royal Naval Air Station, he then fell ill. He died at the Royal Naval Auxiliary Hospital in Sherborne and is buried in the old cemetery at Swanage, beside Northbrook Road, on the north side of the railway line as it approaches the station.

An equally audacious winner of the Victoria Cross was Lieutenant (Admiral Sir) Victor Crutchley (1892-1986) of Mappercombe Manor at Nettlecombe, near Powerstock. He faced great risk on HMS *Centurion* at the Battle of Jutland and then aboard HMS *Brilliant* in the attempt to block Ostend Harbour on 22-23 April 1918. For that action he was awarded the Distinguished Service Cross.

Crutchley returned to Ostend, in the suicidal repeat operation of 9-10 May 1918, as commander of the block-ship HMS *Vindictive* which was stuffed with explosives. The

Swanage gravestone to Dunraven *hero Ernest Pitcher VC.*

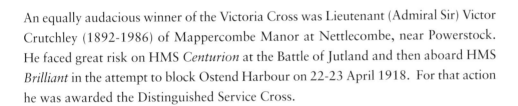

German prisoners arriving in Dorchester.

*Prisoners marching to camp, at
the Royal Horse Artillery
Barracks.*

*German prisoners marching out
of Dorchester to work.*

crew very nearly became part of the sacrifice on that one-way trip into the German guns. The captain, Commander A. E. Godsal had been killed, and his navigator, Lieutenant Sir John Alleyn, seriously wounded. Crutchley took command and proceeded with the mission through thick fog. He narrowly escaped with his life and this time he received not only Britain's highest honour, the Victoria Cross, but the French Croix de Guerre as well.

Between the wars he commanded the 30,600-ton battleship HMS *Warspite* from 1937 to 1940. Then after a spell ashore as the base commander at Devonport he returned to the water to command the Australian Naval Squadron from 1942 to 1944. He was then Flag Officer Gibraltar until the start of a four-decade retirement in 1947. Sir Victor is buried in Powerstock churchyard beneath a striking wooden cross redolent of another age. It is surmounted by the 'For Valour' insignia of the Victoria Cross.

For most young men it would be the trenches rather than the war at sea. One whose story sums up the changing social situation and attitude of the twentieth century was Alec Waugh (1898-1981) who compiled the gay classic *The Loom of Youth* in seven and a half weeks, during the First World War, when he was a 17-year-old pupil at Sherborne School.

The book had to be completed in haste in December 1915 as he was due to sail to the trenches. 'Surely you will fight for King and Country' was the last poster he saw in the London Underground, urging 'Come along, Boys, before it is too late.' Alec posted the manuscript to his father, the Shirburnian author, critic and editor Arthur Waugh (1866-1943), at Hampstead. He was managing director of Chapman and Hall and had just published *Reticence in Literature*. Arthur saw Alec's novel into print in 1917:

'Just after Christmas in 1915 he began The Loom of Youth, *writing it on any odd sheets of paper which he could collect in the hut of the YMCA at Berkhamsted, and sending me the pages to read, morning after morning, between breakfast time and the next parade. He wrote the book with the*

Dorchester Prison Guards' Camp beside Poundbury hill-fort.

*Dorchester POW Camp –
'Kommandant des Kriegsgefangenen Lagers'.*

*Right: Dorchester POW
Camp – 'Camp, 1919'.*
(K. Bartholmay)

Dorchester POW Camp – 'Camp-Eingang bei nacht'.
(Josef Jakob Melzl)

Dorchester POW Camp – 'Bibliother, Postabgabe, Musifbaracke'.
(Josef Jacob Meltzl)

conviction of a man who had a task set before him, and he carried the task through within a period of six weeks. It was a genuine tour de force, done against time.'

Textual changes, such as having the trains for Derbyshire pulling out of Waterloo, resulted from the publisher making last-minute changes to 300 pages of proofs to lessen the chances of a libel action. Sherborne School featured as Fernhurst with fictitious Talbot Baines Reed as its headmaster. The school needed two simple reforms – dismissal of all the masters and expulsion of all the boys. Alec by now was serving with the Dorsetshire Regiment on the Western Front and was taken prisoner of war in 1918. Those who risked life and limb to contend with daily hazards such as a runaway cart in Sherborne's Cheap Street borrowed the language of war to denounce:

'… a traitor to School and Country, despicably unpatriotic.'

Despite the rhetoric, the novel contains no explicit sexual references, and by the standards of the end of the century seemed quite restrained. It would have been more accurate to have described it as subversive. To the uninitiated, or those from a non-public-school background, it was regarded as a celebration of cricket rather than sexuality.

Alec Waugh's boyfriend was named as Arthur. Both were caught and Alec was expelled. The resulting book was banned in Sherborne and boys were promised an immediate beating if they were caught in possession of a copy. As a result, driven underground, it became required reading. 'Put house and school above your personal desires,' headmaster Nowell Charles Smith urged, as he issued an edict forbidding associations between boys of different houses, or with those of a different age. Arthur Waugh sent his second son – Evelyn who was born in 1903 – to Lancing College. Nowell Smith saw it as his duty to maintain the morale of his boys who went to war, as an obituary writer would record:

'Practically every wounded boy in that First War had a letter from him (and there were hundreds) when he was nearly worked to death anyway.'

After devoting a couple of pages to 'heart-broken recrimination' concerning the Waughs, in *A History of Sherborne School*, author A. B. Gourlay summarises the contribution of the rest of the lads to the conflict with brief but poignant statistics:

'One thousand one hundred and fifty-seven Shirburnians in all served in the war. Two of these had won the VC, C. E. Hudson and E. Bamford; there were 58 DSOs, 76 MCs, 157 mentions in despatches and 100 other decorations, British and foreign. Lives lost amounted to 221, approximately equivalent to the whole strength of the school in 1914 – a ratio fairly consistently maintained throughout the country.'

Volunteer soldier Lieutenant Sidney Clayton Woodroffe (1895-1915), from Branksome Park, was posthumously awarded the VC for an action with the Rifle Brigade on the Western Front. The announcement was made on 6 September 1915.

Dorchester POW Camp – 'Prisoner-Garten'.
(Ernst Poche)

Dorchester POW Camp – 'Unter den Kastanien'. (Eric Streuber)

Dorchester POW Camp – 'Obdere d Reihe'. (Ios Walter)

Dorchester POW Camp – 'Traume'. (K. Bartholmay)

Dorchester POW Camp – 'Herbst, 1918'. (Ernst Poche)

HEROES AND PRISONERS

Captain Julian Royds Gribble (1897-1918) of Kingston Russell House, near Long Bredy, died of his wounds while fighting with the Royal Warwicks on the Western Front and was gazetted for the Victoria Cross on 28 June 1918. His father, George James Gribble (1846-1927) had restored Kingston Russell to its former glory.

Steel-nerved Jack Counter from Blandford volunteered on the Western Front for a perilous crawl through no-man's-land and a reconnaissance mission into German lines in 1918. Against all the odds he returned – with the required information – and was rewarded with the VC.

Meanwhile, at home, Dorset saw increasing numbers of German prisoners. In Dorchester the Royal Horse Artillery Barracks (since known as Marabout Barracks) became a Prisoner of War Camp – Kriegsgefangenen Lagers, Dorchester – with its Prison Guards' Camp being established in a tented compound beside the eastern rampart of Poundbury hill-fort. The inmates produced a series of engravings at the end of the war which they dedicated to their Kommandant, H. C. Butterley. Prisoners-of-war were known as 'Kriegies'.

Dorchester POW Camp – 'Gesamtansicht von Lager II'. (Erich Streuber)

Dorchester POW Camp – 'Soldatenheim und Theaterhalle'. (H. Delfs)

Dorchester POW Camp – *'Abend auf der Sperlingshohe.* (K. Bartholmay)

Below: *Dorchester POW Camp* – *'Baracken am Hugel'.* (Ernst Poche)

Dorchester POW Camp – *'Grabmal Deutscher Kriegsgefangener'.* (K. Bartholmay)

Left: *Dorchester POW Camp* – *'Schreibstube vom Lager II'.* (Kurt Polent)

HEROES AND PRISONERS

Two German Prisoner of War camps were established at Blandford where they could be guarded by the nearby Royal Naval Division – followed by the Royal Air Force with its Mechanical Transport Camp in 1918 – and provide it with manpower. Prisoners were also hired out to local farmers.

One camp was at Milldown, half a mile north of the town, which was served by a railway siding from Milldown level-crossing. The other was beside Cuckoo Clump wood at the eastern edge of Blandford Camp.

Four 'Unknown German Soldiers' lie beneath an iron cross in Tarrant Monkton churchyard. They died in the influenza pandemic of 1918-19. Military historian Major Alan Harfield failed to obtain their names from either British or German war graves authorities. He was told that the parson refused to give them a burial service or enter their names in the parish register. Karl Jager and Max Heinitz died in Milldown Camp in 1918, also with virulent influenza, and lie in the military plot at Blandford cemetery, beside the Salisbury road.

twenty one
Red Cross Hospitals

SIXTY DETACHMENTS of the Red Cross in Dorset were registered at the War Office before the declaration of war. Dorchester detachment hosted an annual gathering of volunteers, going through their paces with Boy Scout patients, in the grounds of Colliton House, Dorchester, at the end of July. That war clouds were already forming was shown by the non-attendance – having been summoned to London because of 'the political situation' – of the senior officer who should have made the inspection. Red Cross Voluntary Aid Detachments, comprising 'the cream of England's womanhood', were about to be mobilised.

Crucially, the local detachments were told by Colonel H. Mackey of Southern Command to prepare:

> *'Temporary Hospitals of 50 or more beds and Convalescent Homes, for the overflow of cases from the Military Hospitals receiving casualties from the Expeditionary Force.'*

By 2 September 1914, Colonel John Henry Balguy of Bockhampton, as county director, had organised the provision of:

> *'1,200 beds ready and equipped with complete nursing and trained staffs and medical attendance.'*

Ironically, Brigadier-General Balguy as he became, records in *The Red Cross in Dorset during the War* that their ardour and enthusiasm were dampened by the authorities. This was only a contingency, they were told, and 'we should probably never be used'. Frank Hastings, secretary of the British Red Cross Society, saw them as a measure that would only 'arise in the case of invasion'. Volunteers from Blandford Red Cross Hospital (70 beds) and Iwerne Hospital (20 beds) became so disillusioned that they threatened to resign en mass and offer their services elsewhere.

The president at the time, Mrs Mary Mount-Batten of Up Cerne House, secured the promise of a limited deployment as 'a fresh stimulus to the work generally'. She also donated a 'Mount-Batten Challenge Cup' to promote healthy inter-detachment rivalry. Together with the Countess of Ilchester, from Melbury House – her successor as president – she continued to cajole fellow landowners into placing their homes and gardens, mostly rent-free, at the disposal of the Red Cross for use as hospitals.

Their bureaucracy belonged to another age as the Red Cross chose for its administrative boundaries the 12 Poor Law divisions that historically attached to the county. Each of these groups had a Union work-house though not every one was provided with a hospital. Most were in operation from the autumn of 1914 through to the spring of 1919.

The Red Cross also provided for comforts and needs, but with rationing from the spring of 1918 – when the U-boat campaign disrupted imports – neither the quantity or quality of supplies could be guaranteed, as this note from the county supply depot confirmed:

Red Cross ambulance, from Northamptonshire, photographed at Wells, Somerset.

> *'The chocolate arrived at the depot in bulk, 1,000 pounds a time. It had to be unpacked, weighed out in packets as asked for, and as it was undesirable to break up the cakes, some hospitals got more than they paid for. Also it was never known beforehand what kind of chocolate would be issued, and the last lot received was not appreciated. Matches likewise arrived in bulk, and at the time were very scarce in the country, and three or four packages were lost in transit to the hospitals.'*

Miss Hebe Templer organised 'an army of ladies' to produce a variety of 'in county' products that show the variety of specialist needs that had to be supplied in bulk:

> *'We make tail bandages, roller bandages, swabs and fomentation pads. Moist dressings are also required in large quantities and these use sphagnum moss which is collected by boys from mossy grassland valleys and the heathland moors. Special products include pneumonia jackets, to keep fever victims warm, and trench-foot slippers. Davis slings, stump covers and knee caps have brought home to us the fact that some soldiers have been horribly mutilated. Making vests and pants, and lavender bags to freshen the air, can be almost therapeutic.'*

The war records of Dorset's individual volunteers were recorded on a total of 2,794 pink cards that were forwarded to national headquarters in January 1919. They had cared for a total of 21,200 patients.

In alphabetical order, the Dorset area Red Cross institutions and military hospitals included:

Beaucroft Voluntary Aid Hospital, Wimborne. Owners – executors of the late Mrs Lees. Commandant – Miss Carr-Glyn. Opened in December 1914 with 32 beds for troops billeted nearby and closed for a month on their departure to the Middle East in May 1915. It was then re-opened, as a branch of Cosham Military Hospital, for wounded troops from overseas. It was provided with full surgical facilities and increased to 54 beds. The hospital had the use of a Red Cross ambulance, shared with other local hospitals, and a second vehicle donated for the duration of the war by Dorset Automobile Club.

Branksome Gate Auxiliary Hospital for Officers, Bournemouth. Managed by Lady Dudley.

Bryanston RAF Hospital. Owner – Lord Portman. A large hut, with 75 beds, in Bryanston Park, established in 1918.

Burdon Military Hospital, Weymouth. Leased by the War Office. Medical Officer Commanding – Lieutenant-Colonel E. R. S. Carroll. This was the 'parent' hospital for Dorset's voluntary institutions. Its 'Provisional Limb Ward' supplied amputees with 'Brighton Plaster Pylons' – made by Mrs Dorothy Hanbury – and trained patients to use them. These had been devised by the Orthopaedic Hospital at Brighton. General Balguy and Mr Shury manufactured wooden splints and metal hinges for moving parts which possessed 'great mechanical ability and manual dexterity'. The matron at Weymouth was Miss Schafer. Many hundred wounded Indians were brought to the town by the *Glencart Castle* in 1915. Five motor ambulances were loaned by Australian units stationed in the area.

Castle Voluntary Aid Hospital, Sherborne. Owner – Major and Mrs Wingfield-Digby. Miss M. Goodridge was the sister-in-charge. The hospital was established in Sherborne Castle in 1914 and transferred to The Cedars, Long Street, in March 1916.

The Cedars Voluntary Aid Hospital, Sherborne. Owner – Major Gerald Russell Rickett, surgeon to the Yeatman Hospital, being his home in Long Street. Commandant – Mrs Waldegrave. In use from November 1916. Its medical officer, Dr J. F. L. Whittingdale, gave his services without charge for the duration of the war. The Sherborne group of hospitals had a transport pool of ten motor ambulances, two vans loaned by Sherborne Steam Laundry, and several private cars.

Chantmarle Voluntary Aid Hospital, near Evershot. Owner – Francis Ewart Savile. Commandant – Lady Lilian Digby. In use until November 1915 when it transferred to Holnest Park, near Sherborne.

Chetnole Voluntary Aid Hospital, near Sherborne. Owners and managers – Colonel and Mrs Harvey Alexander, being their home at The Grange. Including marquees it had 30 beds. The medical officer was Dr Stanley Stephens.

Church Street Voluntary Aid Hospital, Dorchester. Owner – Sir Robert Williams MP. Commandant – Mrs Acland. No. 5 Church Street was in use from 1914 until March 1916 when it was merged with Colliton House.

RED CROSS HOSPITALS

Cluny Voluntary Aid Hospital, Swanage. Owners – trustees of the late Kenneth Anderson. Commandant – Dr Baiss. Opened in November 1914, with 50 beds, as the medical facility for troops billeted in the Isle of Purbeck. From September 1915 it received transfers from Cornelia Hospital, Poole, and Mont Dore, Bournemouth. The matron was Miss Henry.

Colliton House Voluntary Aid Hospital, Dorchester. Owner – Colonel and Mrs Hughes-Onslow. Commandant – Miss Marsden. Increased from 40 to 100 beds on absorbing Church Street Hospital. Marquees across the lawn made it a 'very complete hospital' with a first-class operating theatre, an X-ray installation, and Mechano-therapeutic apparatus. T. Lynes organised a motor pool with vehicles loaded by garage owners Channon and Sons, Hannah and Holland, Lott and Walne, and Tilley and Sons. They also loaned the horse ambulance from Dorset County Hospital. Chaplain Canon Hankey and matron Miss M. le G. Whitting.

Colliton House Voluntary Aid Detachment Hospital, Dorchester.

Compton House Voluntary Aid Hospital, near Sherborne. Owners – Colonel and Mrs Goodden. Commandant – Mrs Caroline Goodden. Edith Coffey was the nursing sister. Opened on a small scale in March 1915 and increased to 20 beds in 1917. Mrs Goodden recalled:

'From May to October every fine morning was spent on the recreation ground high up on the hill in the park where the men took their tea, and received friends, afterwards playing tennis and croquet till dark. They had a pony carriage at their disposal which they attended to themselves, and a donkey chair, which was a great source of pleasure to those who had lost a leg.'

Convent Voluntary Aid Hospital, Weymouth. Owners – Roman Catholic Church. Commandant – Miss Gertrude Gray. Established in a wing of the Convent of the Sacred Heart on 29 October 1914. Received injured and sick Belgian refugees, who arrived by sea in the autumn of 1914, and remained open until September 1917. Sisters of the convent acted as cooks and all staffing was found locally.

Cornelia Hospital, Poole. The town's general hospital, named for its benefactor (Cornelia, Lady Wimborne) had a number of 'Temporary Wards' – including huts – for 25 military patients. Miss K. Lindsay was the sister-in-charge. Transport was provided by the 4th Hampshire Volunteer Regiment and Women's Reserve Ambulance Corps.

Crag Head Voluntary Aid Hospital, Bournemouth. Owners – Captain Swithenbank RN and executors of the late G. J. Fenwick. Commandants – Miss Girdleston, followed by Miss Turner. This large house, overlooking the sea, was fitted out with 100 beds. A further 30 were added in 1915 with the acquisition of nearby Moss Close. Then the combined capacity was expanded to a total of 207 beds. It also had a large operating theatre and a wide range of facilities. Transport was provided by Hampshire St John's Ambulance brigade, under Dr Bottomley.

Fifehead Magdalen Voluntary Aid Hospital, near Marnhull. Owner and Commandant – Mrs Percy Browne. Mrs Browne, on her own initiative, fitted out her house as an 8-bed hospital, with 'every comfort', that took convalescent cases from Beaucroft Hospital, Wimborne. She tended a total of 37 patients.

Garden Voluntary Aid Hospital, Upwey. Commandant – Miss E. Ferguson.

Grata Quies Auxiliary Military Hospital, Branksome Park. Owner: Mrs Mounsey-Heysham. Leased by the War Office. Commandant – Miss Bottomley.

Greenhill Voluntary Aid Hospital, Sherborne. Owners – trustees of Sherborne School, and Colonel Bullen. Commandant – Mrs MacAdam. Colonel Bullen's land enabled pioneering 'open air treatment in revolving shelters, which afterwards produced such excellent results'. Overseen by Mrs Hargreaves, these enabled the provision of beds to be increased from 40 to 77. The medical officer, Dr Wilson, collapsed with a mental breakdown in December 1918, causing its closure.

Herbert Convalescent Home, Westbourne. Extensive buildings beside Alumhurst

Herbert Convalescent Home, Westbourne, Bournemouth.

The smoking room in the Herbert Home at Westbourne.

Road, above Alum Chine, this was one of largest recuperation homes in the country and continues in use today as the Herbert Hospital.

Holnest Voluntary Aid Hospital, near Sherborne. Owner – Wanley Ellis Sawbridge-Erle-Drax (rented by Lady Ilchester). Commandant – Lady Lilian Digby. Administered by its matron, Miss E. Dimond. Opened with 50 beds, in Holnest Park, in November 1915. Increased to 100 beds by May 1918 with large marquees in the grounds.

The Hut Voluntary Aid Hospital, Ferndown. War Office facility. Assistant Commandant – Mrs Sturt. Functioned as a clinic and sick-bay, with 17 beds, for troops billeted nearby. Closed on 11 March 1915 with the departure of the men for the Middle East.

Infirmary Voluntary Aid Hospital, Wimborne. Owners – Wimborne and Cranborne Poor Law Union. Commandant – Mrs Sturt, followed by Mrs Lyon, helped by Miss Gladys Pringle. Housed in the infirmary of the Union Workhouse. Opened in March 1915 with 50 beds. By 1917 it also had two outdoor shelters and was coping with 62 patients.

Kingston Maurward Red Cross Supply Depot, near Dorchester. Owner – Cecil Hanbury. The county base for Red Cross operations. Miss J. Findlay was the administrator.

Leweston Manor Voluntary Aid Hospital, near Sherborne. Owners – Mr and Mrs Hamilton Fletcher. Opened on 31 October 1914, with 21 beds, increasing to 68 patients on 27 March 1915 when Mrs Hamilton Fletcher had to close it 'for private reasons'.

The Lodge Auxiliary Hospital for Officers, Parkstone. Managed by Lady Dudley.

Lulworth Voluntary Aid Hospital, West Lulworth. Owner – Daniel Radcliff. Commandant – Mrs Robson. The medical facility for troops camped at Lulworth from 25 October to 8 December 1914. Beds for 11 patients. It treated 22 cases.

Massandra Voluntary Aid Hospital, Weymouth. Owner – R. Elworthy. Commandant – Mrs Fraser. Opened on 29 October 1914, with 12 patients, and increased to 40 beds by December 1915. Then large marquees were erected in the garden which overlooks the sea, enabling it to handle 75 patients. Dr Saunderson-Wells was the medical officer.

Mere Voluntary Aid Hospital, Wiltshire. Owners – Church of England Schools. Commandant – Mrs Troyte-Bullock. Housed in Grove Buildings. This opened on 18 October 1914 and had 56 beds. It was administered as part of the Shaftesbury group.

Mont Dore Military Hospital, Bournemouth. Leased by the War Office. Major facility in the former Sanatorium that became the Town Hall.

Hospital humour in cartoons by Private J. H. Dowd.

The Mount Auxiliary Hospital for Officers, Parkstone. Managed by Lady Dudley.

Newton Voluntary Aid Hospital, near Wimborne. Leased house at Newton Peveril, Sturminster Marshall. Commandant – Miss Cross, followed by Miss Anne Wavell and Mrs Tory. Expanded from 15 beds, in December 1914, to 35 beds with a marquee in the garden. This was swept by fire in the summer of 1917. The heroine was Miss Agnes Kent, a nurse, who ventured into the flames to make sure that all the beds were empty.

Plank House Voluntary Aid Hospital, Gillingham. Owner – Henry Wyld. Commandant: – Mrs Charlton Cross, followed by Lady Parr and the Honourable Mrs Austruther. Took troops from Codford Military Hospital and those billeted around Sutton Veny, Wiltshire. Opened 5 November 1914 with 12 patients but soon expanded to 24 beds. Medical officer Dr Farnfield and the matron Mrs Farnfield.

Princess Christian Hospital, Weymouth. Provided operating theatres for the Weymouth group of hospitals.

The Retreat Voluntary Aid Hospital, Shaftesbury. Commandant – Dr Harold Utterton Gould. Six beds were provided in Westminster Cottage Hospital and Dr Gould fitted 16 into his nearby home at Castle Hill House, Bimport. Opened 14 December 1914.

Ryme Voluntary Aid Hospital, Weymouth. Owners – committee of GFS Lodge. Commandant – Miss R. Sneyd-Kinnersley. Having opened with 20 beds on 29 October 1914, in the Lodge meeting room, this moved to Ryme – a large house overlooking Portland Harbour – in July 1915. There it had 32 beds. Accommodation increased to 40 patients, in 1918, with some being in marquees and bell-tents in the garden. The medical officer was Captain Croker-Fox with Miss M. Suffield the sister-in-charge.

St Giles House Voluntary Aid Hospital, Wimborne St Giles. Owners – Lord and Lady Shaftesbury, who donated the north wing of their stately home. Commandant – Miss Lucas. Initial accommodation for 20 patients was increased to 30 beds. In use from 11 January to 17 July 1915, during which it treated 72 patients.

St John's Voluntary Aid Hospital, Weymouth. Owners – Vicar and Churchwardens. Commandant – Mrs Gordon-Steward. Opened in St John's Mission Room, with 26 beds for Belgian refugees in January 1916, but moved to a large house in Glendinning Avenue which increased its capacity to 38 patients.

Sandacres Private Hospital for Officers, Parkstone. Provided and financed by Sir Ernest Cassel of Branksome Dene.

Sherborne Castle Voluntary Aid Hospital – see entry for Castle Voluntary Aid Hospital. Sherborne. Owner – Major and Mrs Wingfield-Digby. In use until November 1916 when it transferred to The Cedars in Long Street, Sherborne.

South Lytchett Manor Voluntary Aid Hospital, near Poole. Owners – Benita, Lady Lees. Opened on 2 November 1914 and closed on 7 August 1915. Attached to Cosham Military Hospital, it received repatriated wounded from overseas, and treated a total of 136 men.

Springfield Auxiliary Hospital for Officers, Parkstone. Managed by Lady Dudley.

Station Road Voluntary Aid Hospital, Gillingham. Leasehold houses. Commandant – Mrs Leatham, who was succeeded by her daughter, Miss Leatham. Opened on 20 October 1914 with 20 patients and expanded to 62 beds by May 1918.

Stourfield House Sanatorium, Southbourne. A Bournemouth mansion converted by the British Legion into a sanatorium for crippled and convalescent soldiers. It was renamed Douglas House as a tribute to Field-Marshal Sir Douglas Haig.

Sturminster Voluntary Aid Hospital, Sturminster Newton. Owner – Board of Guardians. Commandant – Mrs Whatman, succeeded by Miss Audrey Charlesworth. Housed 25 patients in the former Union Workhouse.

Trent Voluntary Aid Hospital, near Sherborne. Owner – Mrs Hichens. This was her home, Flamberts, in Rigg Lane. Opened in March 1915, with 20 convalescent beds, but upgraded to a Class-A hospital from March to August 1917.

Weymouth Military Hospital – see entry for Burdon Military Hospital, Weymouth.

Wimborne Cottage Hospital. Three beds were reserved for military patients.

Wincanton Voluntary Aid Hospital, Somerset. Owners – Roman Catholic Church. Housed in the Priory, South Street, this was administered as part of the Sherborne group.

Woodlyn Private Hospital for Officers, Branksome Park. Managed by Lady Carter.

Yeatman Civil Hospital, Sherborne. Had several service wards, managed by Sister Kearwell.

Yeovil Voluntary Aid Hospital, Somerset. Housed in the Baptist School, in the Somerset town, this was administered as part of the Sherborne group.

Yetminster Voluntary Aid Hospital, near Sherborne. Owners – Mr and Mrs Arthur Williams, being their home at Hill House. Transferred to Chetnole early in the war.

22

After Armageddon

THE FIRST NEWS of the Armistice to reach Dorset was a wireless message from Paris to the Royal Naval Airship Station at Powerstock at 06.30 hours on 11 November 1918. This was followed by the official notification from the Admiralty. The following Naval signal was telegraphed from the Flag Officer, Portland, at 07.45 hours, to 'All Units, Royal Navy and Royal Marines' in the Portland Command Area:

> *'Hostilities will cease at 11.00 hrs to-day Nov. 11th AAA*
>
> *All precautions are to be preserved and there will be no communication with the Enemy AAA All units are to report dispositions and to remain at a state of readiness to meet any demand AAA*
>
> *Further instructions will be issued regarding enemy units, especially submarines, now at sea AAA*
>
> *Acknowledge AAA'*

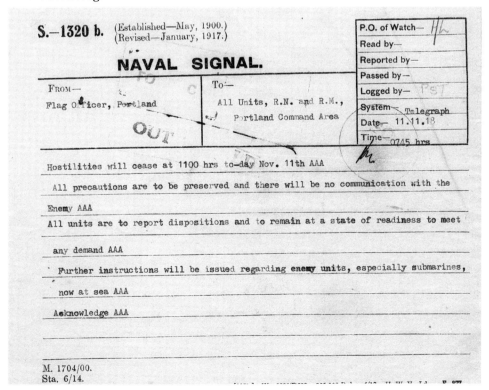

Armistice Day signal from the Flag Officer, Portland.

The day after the Armistice – 12 November 1918 – being celebrated at Weymouth.

Church bells were rung and town centres in Bournemouth, Bridport, Dorchester, Poole and Weymouth filled with thousands of people who wanted to celebrate. Bigger ad hoc ceremonies following at lunchtime on 12 November by which time every available band in the county had taken to the streets.

Among the surrendered submarines that put into Portland Harbour was *U-10* which went on display in Hope Cove, Weymouth.

Surrendered German submarine U-10 at Hope Cove, Weymouth.

AFTER ARMAGEDDON

Japanese warships at Poole Quay after difficulties towing a former German U-boat to the Far East, in January 1919.

An echo of past dangers came at dawn on 8 January 1919 when lifeboat maroons at Poole signalled that the surrendered German submarine *U-143* was aground on the Hook Sands with a southerly gale blowing inshore from Poole Bay and waves breaking across the boat. *U-143* was en route to Japan – a British ally in the First World War – as part of German reparations. Travelling down the Channel, she had come into the bay with engine trouble while her two escorts, the Japanese destroyers *Kanran* and *Kashiwa*, stood by offshore, not daring to venture closer into disturbed and shallow waters.

The Royal Navy sent the drifter HMT *Wild Oak* from Portland to give assistance but her draught also proved too deep for making a close approach. In mid-morning the naval drifter entered Poole Harbour to tow the lifeboat *Harmar* out through the Sandbanks gap against a strengthening gale and surging tide. They then had a mile to go before the lifeboatmen could begin to row their way to the stricken submarine as it rolled in the rising water. Meanwhile the tug *Commerce* approached the U-boat from the east with lines for the lifeboat to attach. These proved useless so the destroyer *Kanran*, with stronger cables, took over from the tug.

By now it was nightfall, and all rescue efforts had failed, but the Japanese crew stubbornly refused to quit the submarine. That night a further series of distress rockets diverted the *Harmar*'s attention, westwards to a motor schooner in difficulties between the Hook Sands and Sandbanks. *Zwaluw*, from Antwerp, had dragged her anchors and was being driven ashore towards Canford Cliffs. Her crew were eventually taken off and reached Poole Quay at 03.30 hours on 9 January 1919.

The Japanese seamen aboard the submarine at last made radio contact with Tokyo, via the destroyers, and were reassured that drowning was a compulsory part of the job description. The *Harmar* was recalled from Poole but it took another 12 hours before the combination of the lifeboat and the *Wild Wave* beat their way out again to the Hook Sands. There the 28 beleaguered submariners were taken off, in fading light, at 17.50 hours on the 9th.

One of the destroyers entered Poole Harbour so that the men could be transferred from the lifeboat in the calmer waters of Brownsea Road anchorage. As for *U-143*, after the Japanese warships waited at Poole Quay for a week, the submarine was towed off the sandbank by tugs during the next sequence of optimum tides. In vindication of German engineering, she had only suffered a few dents, and the ocean voyage resumed.

The war's final fling was into Russia where the British Government supported White Russian resistance against Bolshevist revolutionaries. One of these 'Provisional Units' of the Russian Relief Force was drawn from the West Country. It included nine officers and 200 other ranks of the 1st Battalion, Dorsetshire Regiment, plus 40 men from the 2nd Dorsets. Their commander, in May 1919, was Captain C. H. Woodhouse, who had just been released from internment in Holland. Captain Wheeler was second in command. They reported to Crowborough Camp, Sussex, and joined 238th Special Brigade under Brigadier-General George William St George Grogan VC (1875-1962).

They sailed from Tilbury on 11 May and broke through the ice in the Barents Sea, off Murmansk, to reach Archangel in the White Sea on the 27th. Steamers towed them in barges to Dwina, in dense pinewoods, and the front at Kurgomen. Much marching and many dead mules later, after struggling through swampy forests and melting tundra, they found their objectives at Topsa and Troitza had been evacuated by the Bolsheviks. Before the units could move on towards Selmenga, the Dorset company was diverted to Ust Pinega, towards Archangel, where their White Russian allies had mutinied.

Poole Park field gun display-piece from the Western Front.

That had dissolved by the time they arrived, and the Dorsets were moved to the next problem place, where they did at least exchange a few shells with Bolsheviks. One man was killed on 27 July 1919. By early September the visitors had moved on to Yemtsa but again found that the war tended to dissolve ahead of them. The plug was pulled on the uneventful adventure. They were to leave Russia before the Arctic winter set in. Having departed from Archangel on 27 September, the men were back at Crowborough on 8 October.

Meanwhile, back in Dorchester, Lieutenant-Colonel Hannay had been reconstructing the main force of the 1st Battalion, Dorsetshire Regiment. 'Home Rule' was threatening to split the United Kingdom of Britain and Ireland. There the 3rd Battalion was holding nationalist Donegal and the divided city of Londonderry 'in aid of the civil power'. On 15 August 1919, 200 men came under a barrage of stones and bottles from rioters, as another 200 tried to quell the looting of city centre shops. On a lighter note, the Dorsets won the Irish Command Cricket Championship.

Colonel Hannay retired in May 1920 and was succeeded by Lieutenant-Colonel Moulton-Barrett. The 2nd Battalion remained in Ireland after the 'Peace Treaty' had been signed by Colonial Secretary Winston Churchill for the British and General Michael Collins for the Irish in January 1922. Their Londonderry garrison had not been included in Eire – the Irish Free State – and the 2nd Dorsets did not return to Malplaquet Barracks, Aldershot, until 12 September 1922.

AFTER ARMAGEDDON

Of the 370 emaciated men of the 2nd Battalion, Dorsetshire Regiment, who passed into Turkish hands at Kut al Amara, Mesopotamia, only about 70 survived the marching, misery and starvation. The *Dorset County Chronicle* records that the final Dorchester 'Kut Day' held by the Dorset Kut Relief Fund was rounded off 'by entertaining at dinner the sadly small remnant of the battalion who have returned to England'. It took place in the Town Hall at Dorchester on 25 February 1919. Entertainment was provided by the Frampton Family Band with pianoforte items by W. R. Hurst.

The survivors – 'the gallant fifty-one, with a bugle band at their head' – marched from Depot Barracks, along the Bridport Road and down High East Street from Top o' Town, to North Square. The town's streets were 'gaily beflagged'. There were three officers who had been at Kut – Major-General Sir Walter Delamain, Lieutenant-Colonel G. M. Herbert, and Captain S. W. Miller. The list collected by the newspaper reporter gives a total of 52 other ranks:

> *'Private G. S. Abbott, Private J. Adams, Private G. Angus, Private G. Allen, Sgt G. Barfoot, Private Barrett DCM, Private A. Barrow, Sgt Briers, L-Corp E. Burt, Private Burwood, Private W. J. Butcher, Private W. J. Butler, Private F. Carter, Corp F. Castaldini, L-Corp G. Cole, Private W. Cole, CSM J. R. Cox, Private H. C. Cullum, Private J. Cyer, RQMS de Lara DCM, CSM R. Dibbs, Private W. C. Diffey, CQMS H. Drew, Corp Duthie, Private W. H. Foster, Sgt W. Furrmage, Private Gibbs, RQMS F. A. Harvey, Private G. Knight, Private R. J. Legg, CQMS Maidment DCM, Private A. Methuen, Private E. Moth, Private Mumford, Private W. Norman, Private A. E. Pearce, Private W. Piper, Private F. W. Pollard, Private W. Rabey, Private G. Roff, Private C. Ryder, Corp Scott, Corp H. Shaw, Private W. J. Sherlock, L-Corp A. Stanley, Private W. F. Studd, Private J. Tilsed, Private W. Turner, Private J Wadman, Private Wheeler, L-Corp J. Williams and Private T. Wright.'*

Captain A. D. Pass from Wootton Fitzpaine, responding to the loyal toast, said he was glad of the chance of having a dig at the Turk, for although he did not have the honour to be in Kut, yet he was the guest of the Turks – from Gallipoli – longer than any of those present that evening. People at home, he said, often thought they were fortunate to be the prisoners of such gentleman. He did not pull his punch when it came to explaining how, of the 6,000 missing who were expected to turn up as prisoners from Mesopotamia, there were only 17 officers and 300 men:

> *'What happened to the rest? They were just murdered, and there is plenty of evidence forthcoming to prove it. As one of the small band of Gallipoli survivors, I should like to bear record to the reputation which the 5th Dorsets made for themselves when they first went into action in Gallipoli. The Dorset Yeomanry arrived about a fortnight after the first Suvla Bay landing, and they were continually stopped by troops of different regiments with the remark – "You Dorsets have something to live up to here for the 5th Dorsets have made a name for themselves".'*

W. S. Edwards, the Mayor of Bridport, described local efforts for the Kut Relief Fund and said that the previous evening there had been a meeting about erecting his town's war memorial, with the following wording being agreed:

'Greater love hath no man than this that he lay down his life for his friends.'

He also referred to current labour unrest and strikes and said that the 'only way to ensure peace, prosperity, and happiness is by good, honest hard work'. Major-General Delamain – rising to regimental shouts of 'Good old 16th Brigade' – told his men:

'It is very nice to see you sitting down to a square meal instead of picking the bones of an old mule.'

General Delamain said many would be surprised to hear him praise 'the patience and kindness of German officers' who had interceded on the prisoners' behalf with the Turks, and also defended his Indian troops from 'a gross libel' about their conduct, which had been exemplary.

The Treaty of Versailles was signed on 29 June 1919 – five years to the day after the assassination of Archduke Ferdinand which had been the catalyst for the conflict – and King George V declared a National Thanksgiving Day on 6 July 1919. Colonel Hannay took the regimental colours from Londonderry to Dorset, for a memorial service in Sherborne Abbey, on 18 September 1919.

Portland stone graves to men of the British Empire, in Sarre Road Cemetery No. 2, where the Battle of the Somme began on 1 July 1916.

Dorset featured in the lasting memorials to 'The Glorious Dead'. The design for nearly a million white gravestones was clinched by the poet Rudyard Kipling who argued the case for a secular-shaped slab of Portland stone rather than the conventional cross, as chosen by the French, and persuaded Major-General Fabian Ware of the War Graves Commission. Having lost his son, John, to the war, Kipling came up with the tender wording for unidentified graves. They were to be an airman, sailor or and soldier of the Great War, 'known unto God'.

Their national memorial was to be the grave of the 'Unknown Soldier', represented by one of their number chosen by lot, in Westminster Abbey. A roadside gathering point for Armistice commemorations was to be the Cenotaph – the Greek word for an empty tomb – outside the War Office at the widest point in Whitehall. Its monumental equivalent in the battlefields of the Western Front is the Menin Gate, in Portland stone, with panels listing the names of those who have no known grave.

The London Cenotaph was initially built in wood to a blueprint by architect Sir Edwin Lutyens. The permanent version that superseded it, again in Portland stone, was dedicated to 'Our Glorious Dead' by King George V on 11 November 1921. An inspired touch to the design was that it has no vertical parallel lines. The sides incline slightly, giving the illusion of greater height – it is only 35 feet high – and project towards a focal-point in the sky. Professor Derwent designed the 5-feet diameter laurel wreaths and the monument was erected by Holland, Hannen & Cubitt Limited. Masons carved the 120 tons of stone in Cubitt's yard at Nine Elms.

The hole in the ground from which it came lies on the south side of the railway cutting across the top of the island, at Above Combe and Pitts Ground, on the opposite side of the road from Pennsylvania Castle. The quarry is two enclosures away from 1640-dated Avice's Cottage and its Portland Museum. David Pushman documented the story in *Precious Stone of Dorset* in 1987.

The Dorset village memorial that is arguably the most beautiful is that at Briantspuddle which was commissioned by Sir Ernest Debenham and designed and carved by the sculptor Eric Gill. It features a Madonna and Child, and Christ, in Purbeck stone and commemorates the dead of department store owner Debenham's pioneering agricultural experiment, his Bladen Estate. Seven men did not return. Topographical writer Arthur Mee found the words 'strangely put but fine philosophy':

Edwin Lutyens chose Portland stone for the national Cenotaph to 'The Glorious Dead' in London's Whitehall.

> *'It is sooth that sin is cause of all this pain*
> *But all shall be well*
> *And all manner of things shall be well.'*

Gill, personally, was strangeness itself in his proclivities and ways. He had a short Dorset war, having passed through Blandford Camp in September 1918, on conscription into the Royal Air Force. Having lost his beard, he was sent to the Mechanical Transport Camp, as a driver. Describing it as 'an utterly unfriendly and unchristian place' he found 'a terrible lot of waiting around' as the war wound down and its last decimations came from disease rather than conflict.

Gill's brother, Kenneth, had been 'a life thrown away' in an air crash in France. Eric at Blandford was more fortunate in being hospitalised with influenza and being able to walk away from the problem. The RAF Camp was particularly hard hit by the pandemic. Twenty-nine of the victims died; the majority being young men from the Recruits Wing. Gill was discharged in November 1918 and never again went beardless. 'Nation shall speak peace unto nation,' he would engrave in his own typographical lettering on the wall of Broadcasting House. He designed the classic sans-serif typeface that carries his name.

Mound of flowers covering the plinth of the memorial beside Sherborne Abbey.

Such sentiments and monuments drew a line under what futurist Herbert George Wells (1866-1946) had optimistically dubbed, in the title of a book published in 1914:

> *'The War that will end War.'*

Both militarism and pacifism now had their place in the sun across the land. Numerous guns and even the occasional tank were mounted in parks or as gate-guards at camps and public buildings. The community lamented its lost generation, mourned especially by mothers and lovers, many of whom would now remain spinsters. This suited a society with a shortage of available men. Most of the military establishments were consolidated into peacetime roles. Though the airships and airmen were stood down, permanent camps continued at Blandford, Bovington, Wyke, Dorchester and Lulworth. So too did the naval base at Portland and the munitions works at Holton Heath and Wyke Regis. The moment of closure for Army veterans came on 8 December 1928 when the Great War colours of the 1st, 2nd, 3rd, 4th, 5th and 6th Battalions of the Dorsetshire Regiment were dedicated and laid up in Sherborne Abbey, where they hang together in the Lady Chapel.